Hal Leonard Student Piano Library

All-In-One Piano Lessons Book A

Authors
Barbara Kreader, Fred Kern, Phillip Keveren, Mona Rejino

Consultants
Tony Caramia, Bruce Berr, Richard Rejino

Manager, Educational Piano
Jennifer Linn

Editor　　　　*Illustrator*
Anne Wester　　Fred Bell

To access audio visit:
www.halleonard.com/mylibrary

Enter Code
6094-0153-3340-7172

ISBN 978-1-4234-8434-9

7777 W. BLUEMOUND RD. P.O. BOX 13819 MILWAUKEE, WI 53213

Copyright © 2009 by HAL LEONARD CORPORATION
International Copyright Secured   All Rights Reserved

For all works contained herein:
Unauthorized copying, arranging, adapting, recording, Internet posting, public performance,
or other distribution of the printed or recorded music in this publication is an infringement of copyright.
Infringers are liable under the law.

Visit Hal Leonard Online at
www.halleonard.com

FOREWORD

The **All-In-One Piano Lessons Books A and B** combine selected pages from the Piano Lessons, Technique, Solos, Theory Workbook, and Practice Games into one easy-to-manage book. Upon completion of the **All-In-One Piano Lessons Books A and B**, students will be ready to continue into Level 2 of the **Hal Leonard Student Piano Library**.

When music excites our interest and imagination, we eagerly put our hearts into learning it. The music in the **Hal Leonard Student Piano Library** encourages practice, progress, confidence, and best of all – success! Over 1,000 students and teachers in a nationwide test market responded with enthusiasm to the:

- variety of styles and moods
- natural rhythmic flow, singable melodies and lyrics
- "best ever" teacher accompaniments
- improvisations integrated throughout the **Lesson Books**
- orchestrated accompaniments included in audio and MIDI formats.

When new concepts have an immediate application to the music, the effort it takes to learn these skills seems worth it. Test market teachers and students were especially excited about the:

- "realistic" pacing that challenges without overwhelming
- clear and concise presentation of concepts that allows room for a teacher's individual approach
- uncluttered page layout that keeps the focus on the music.

The **Hal Leonard Student Piano Library** is the result of the efforts of many individuals. We extend our gratitude to all the teachers, students and colleagues who shared their energy and creative input. May this method guide your learning as you bring this music to life.

Best wishes,

Barbara Kreader   Fred Kern   Phillip Keveren   Mona Rejino

CONTENTS

BLACK-KEY GROUPS

*✓   **Page No.**   **Audio Tracks**

	Title	Description	Page No.	Audio Tracks
___	Sitting At The Piano	*hand position*	4	
___	Feel The Beat!	*understanding pulse*	5	1/2/3
___	Feel The Beat! (Activity Page)		6	
___	Finger Numbers	*L.H., R.H*	7	
___	Number That Finger!		8	
___	The Piano Keyboard		9	
___	Two Black Keys		10	
___	Grandfather's Clock		11	4/5
___	Climbing Up	R.H. = ♩ L.H. = 𝅗𝅥	12	6/7
___	Climbing Down		13	
___	My Own Song	*improvising on two black keys*	14	8
___	Three Black Keys		15	
___	My Dog, Spike	♩ 𝄽	16	9/10
___	Sorry, Spike		17	
___	Party Cat's Bubbles		18	
___	Notes		19	
___	My Dog, Spike (Activity Page)		20	9
___	Left or Right?		21	
___	Merrily We're Off To School	𝅝	22	11/12
___	Merrily We're Off To School (Activity Page)		24	11
___	Long Shadows		25	13/14
___	My Best Friend	♩	26	15/16
___	I Can Do It!	*bars, bar lines*	27	17/18
___	I Can Do It! (Activity Page)		28	
___	Which Hand Plays?		29	
___	Let's Get Silly!	𝄽	30	19/20
___	Drawing Rests		32	
___	Rhythm Detective		33	
___	Water Lily		34	21/22
___	Mister Machine		35	23/24
___	Walking The Dog		36	25/26
___	Night Shadows		37	27/28
___	Night Shadows (Activity Page)		38	27
___	Rhythm Composer	:‖	39	

* Students can check pieces as they play them.

WHITE-KEY GROUPS

			Page No.	Audio Tracks
___	Alphabet Soup	*A B C D E F G*	40	29
___	The Musical Alphabet		41	
___	The Attic Stairs		42	30/31
___	CDE Groups		43	
___	CDE Groups (Activity Page)		44	
___	My Own Song	*improvising on C D E*	45	32
___	Finding CDE On The Keyboard		46	
___	Balloon Ride	*p*, sustain pedal	47	33/34
___	Party Cat	*f*	48	35/36
___	CDE Imagine & Create		49	36/34
___	Make A Party Game		50	
	Party Game Cards		51	
___	FGAB Groups		53	
___	FGAB Groups (Activity Page)		54	
___	My Own Song	*improvising on F G A B*	55	37
___	Monster Under My Bed		56	38/39
___	Finding FGAB On The Keyboard		57	
___	Taxi Tangle		58	40/41
___	Undersea Voyage		59	42/43
___	Sea (C) Song	4/4	60	44/45
___	Rain, Rain, Go Away		61	46/47
___	Dakota Melody		62	48/49
___	Loud Or Soft?		63	
___	Naming Notes On The Keyboard		64	
___	Quiet Night		66	50/51
___	Knock-Knock Joke		67	52/53
___	Knock-Knock Joke (Activity Page)		68	52
___	Old MacDonald Had A Band		70	54/55
___	Rhythm Jam		72	
___	Step Or Repeat		73	
___	Playing Catch		74	56/57
___	Popcorn		75	58/59
___	Bear Dance		76	60/61
___	Stomp Dance		78	62/63
___	Certificate		80	

* Students can check pieces as they play them.

SITTING AT THE PIANO

Ask yourself:

Am I sitting tall but staying relaxed?

Are my wrists and elbows level with the keys of the piano?

HAND POSITION

1) Let your arms hang relaxed at your sides. Notice how your hands stay gently curved.

2) Keep your hands relaxed and curved as you raise them to the piano keyboard.

3) When you are playing the piano, keep your fingers in this relaxed, curved position.

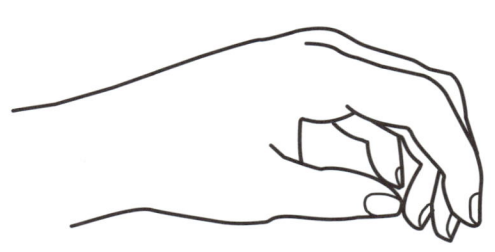

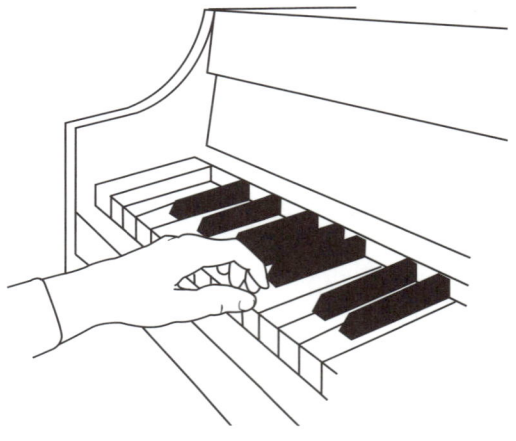

Feel The Beat!

Become aware of the heartbeat inside your body. Feel how it beats in an even pulse. Sometimes your heart beats fast, like when you run; sometimes it beats slowly, like when you are asleep, but it always beats evenly.

Rhythm In Music

Music has a pulse, too. Just like your heartbeat, musical pulse can go fast or slow.

Clap this pulse as your teacher plays the accompaniment below three different times at different speeds:

1) at a slow speed,   2) at a medium speed,   3) at a fast speed.

You can also play this pulse on the piano using any black key. Remember to keep the pulse even.

Accompaniments may also be played using the audio. The numbers indicate the track number.

🔊 1/2/3

Accompaniment

Feel the Beat!
(Activity Page)

Sit quietly and listen to your heartbeat.
Feel how it beats with a steady pulse.

1. Circle the things that have a steady beat.

2. Draw a picture of something that makes a steady, ticking sound.

FINGER NUMBERS

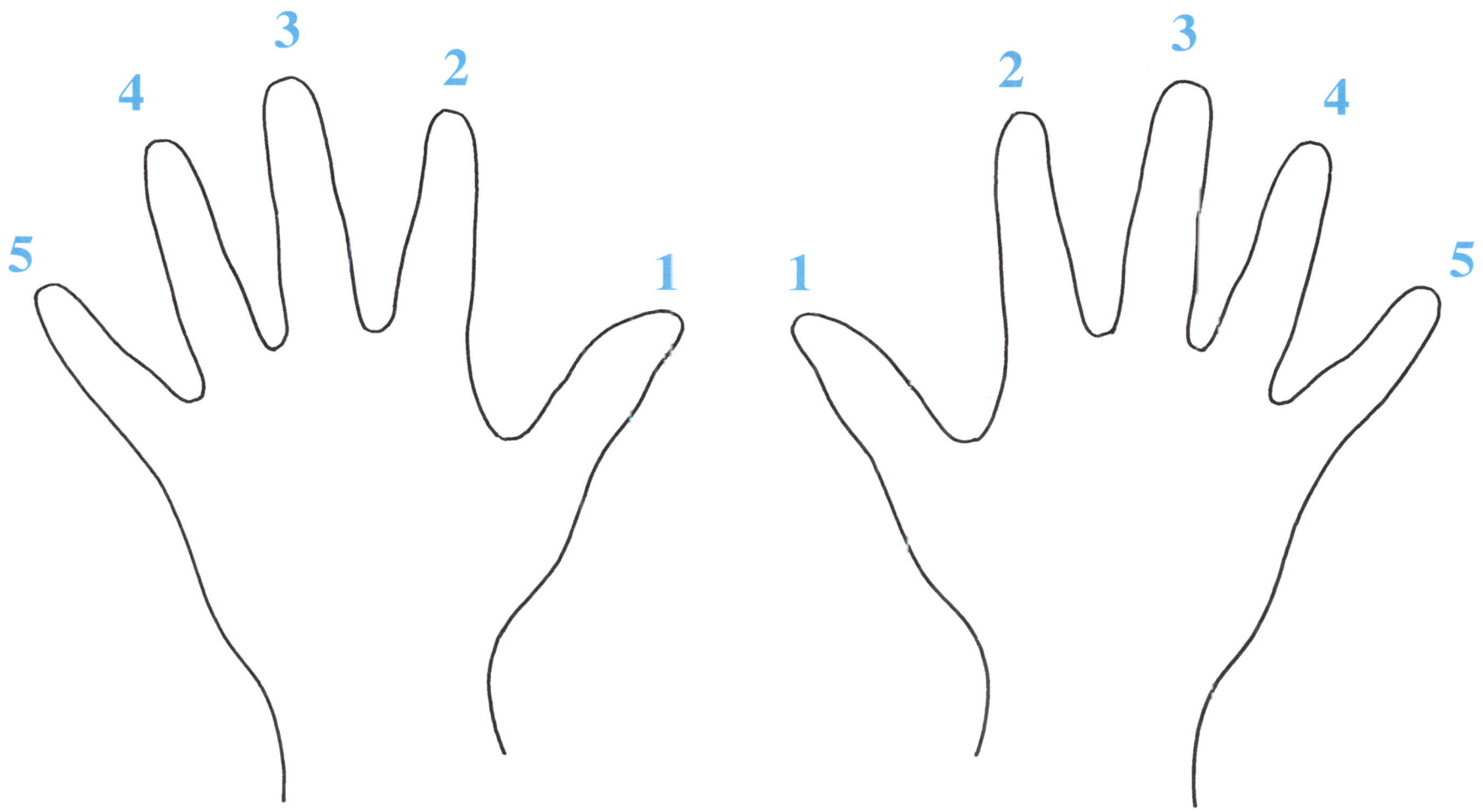

Place your hands together with fingertips touching.

Tap your 1st fingers (thumbs).
Tap your 2nd fingers.
Tap your 3rd fingers.
Tap your 4th fingers.
Tap your 5th fingers.

Tap 4s,　　　tap 2s,　　　tap 5s,　　　tap 1s,　　　tap 3s.

Number That Finger!

Which fingers are wearing the rings?
Write the correct finger number in each box.

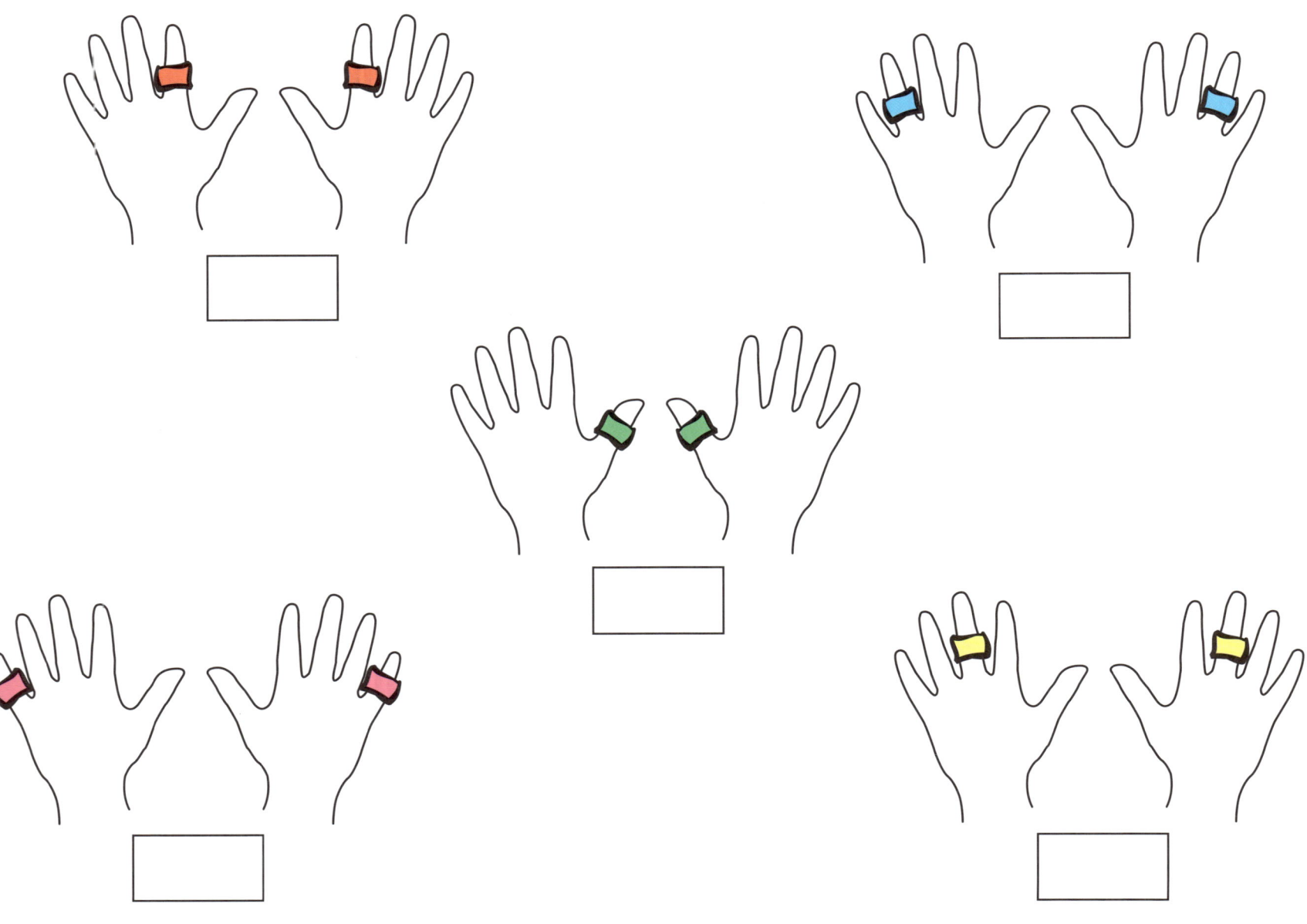

THE PIANO KEYBOARD

The piano keyboard is divided into sets of two and three black keys.

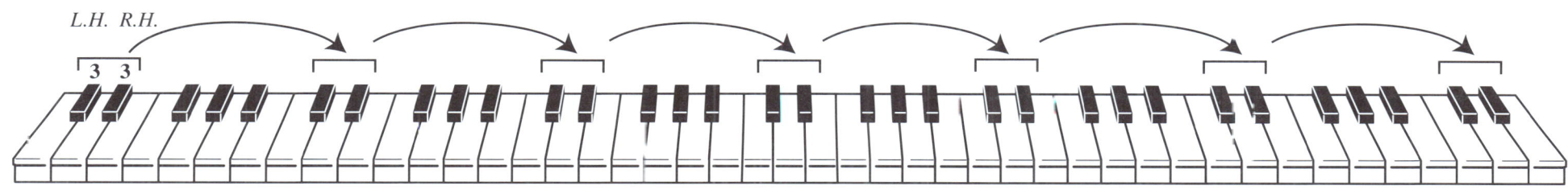

Low   **High**

TWO BLACK KEYS

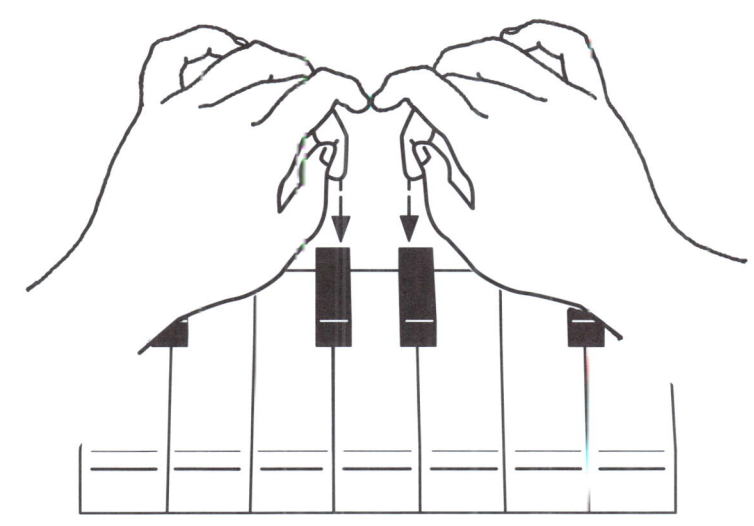

Put your thumbs behind the first joint of your third fingers and use your third fingers to play the groups of two black keys. Start at the low end of the keyboard and play higher.

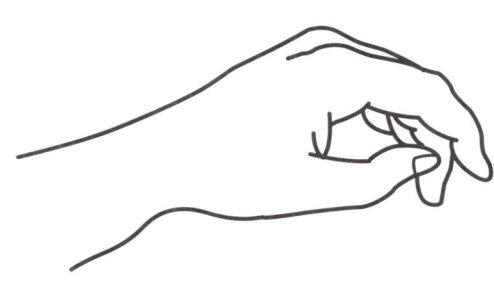

When you play the pieces "Climbing Up" and "Climbing Down" on pages 12 and 13, you will play the groups of two black keys as shown here.

Circle each set of two blackbirds.

Two Black Keys

Colour each set of two black keys.

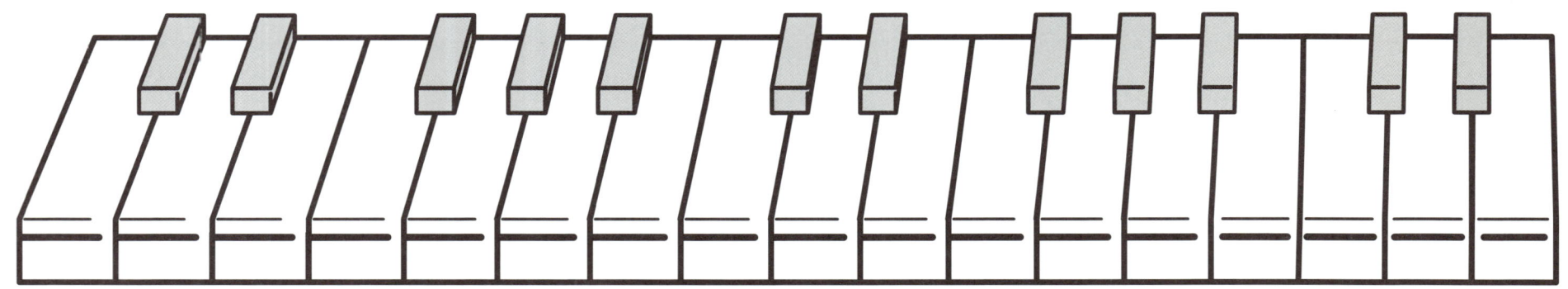

On the piano: Play two black keys way down low.
Play two black keys way up high.

L.H.
R.H.
3 2
2 3

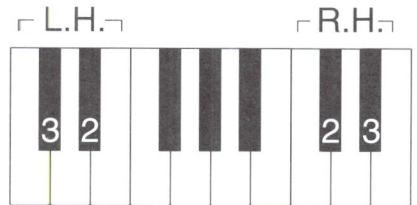

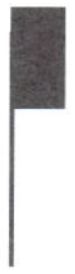

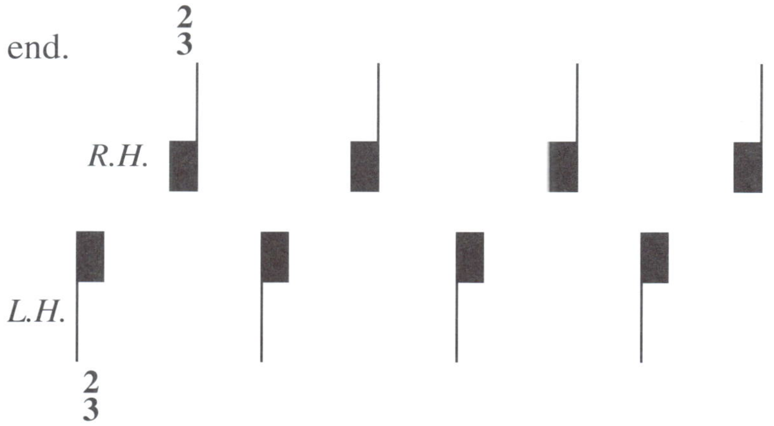

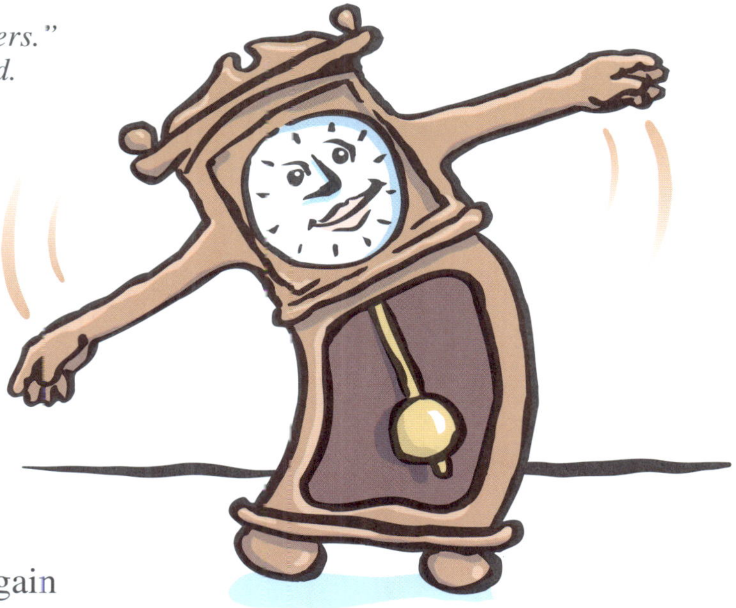

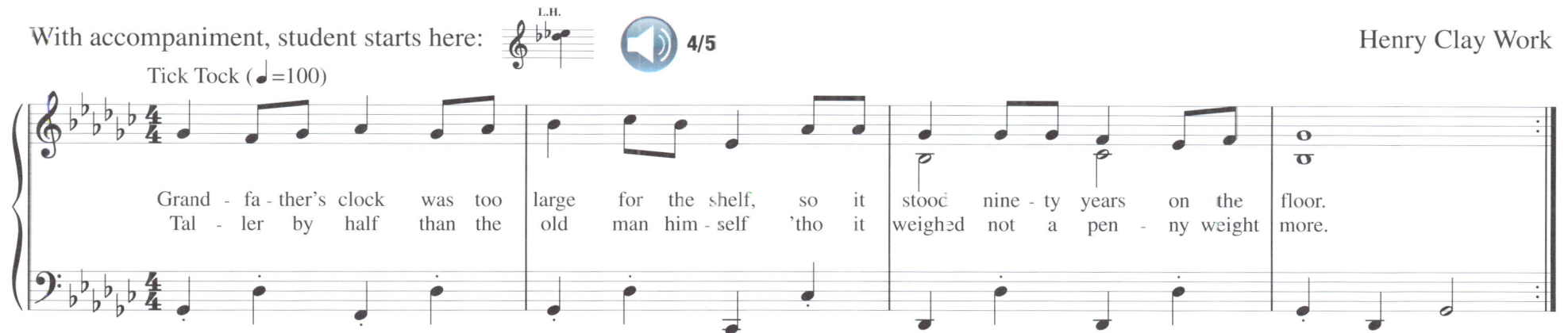

Grandfather's Clock

These small black boxes are called "clusters." Play notes together using fingers indicated.

Keep "ticking" to the end.

2
3
R.H.
L.H.
2
3

Play Again

With accompaniment, student starts here:
L.H.

4/5

Henry Clay Work

Tick Tock (♩=100)
Grand - fa - ther's clock was too large for the shelf, so it stood nine - ty years on the floor.
Tal - ler by half than the old man him - self 'tho it weighed not a pen - ny weight more.

Climbing Up

Two Black Keys
Moving Up The Keyboard

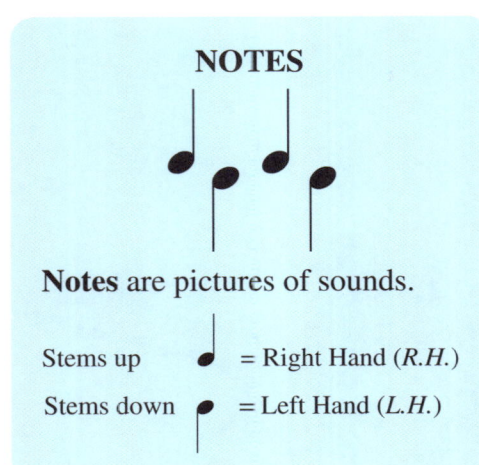

NOTES

Notes are pictures of sounds.

Stems up = Right Hand (*R.H.*)
Stems down = Left Hand (*L.H.*)

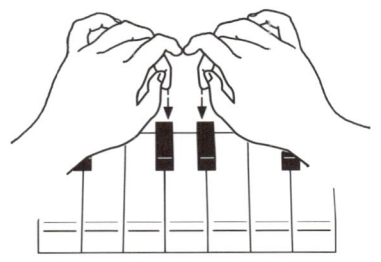

Play this song on two black keys with the third finger in each hand.

It is helpful to clap and sing the words of a piece before playing it. Remember to keep a steady pulse!

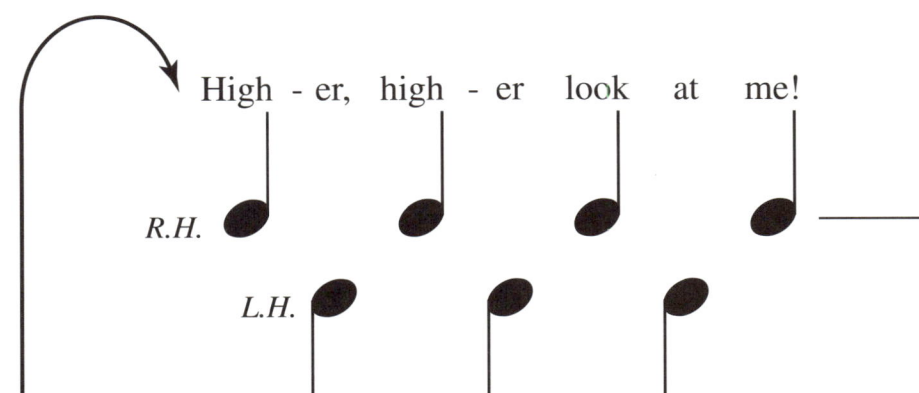

High - er, high - er look at me!

R.H.

L.H.

Climb - ing, climb - ing up this tree,

R.H.

L.H.

With accompaniment, student starts here: 🔊 6/7

With determination (♩ = 120)

mf

8va -

Climbing Down

Two Black Keys
Moving Down The Keyboard

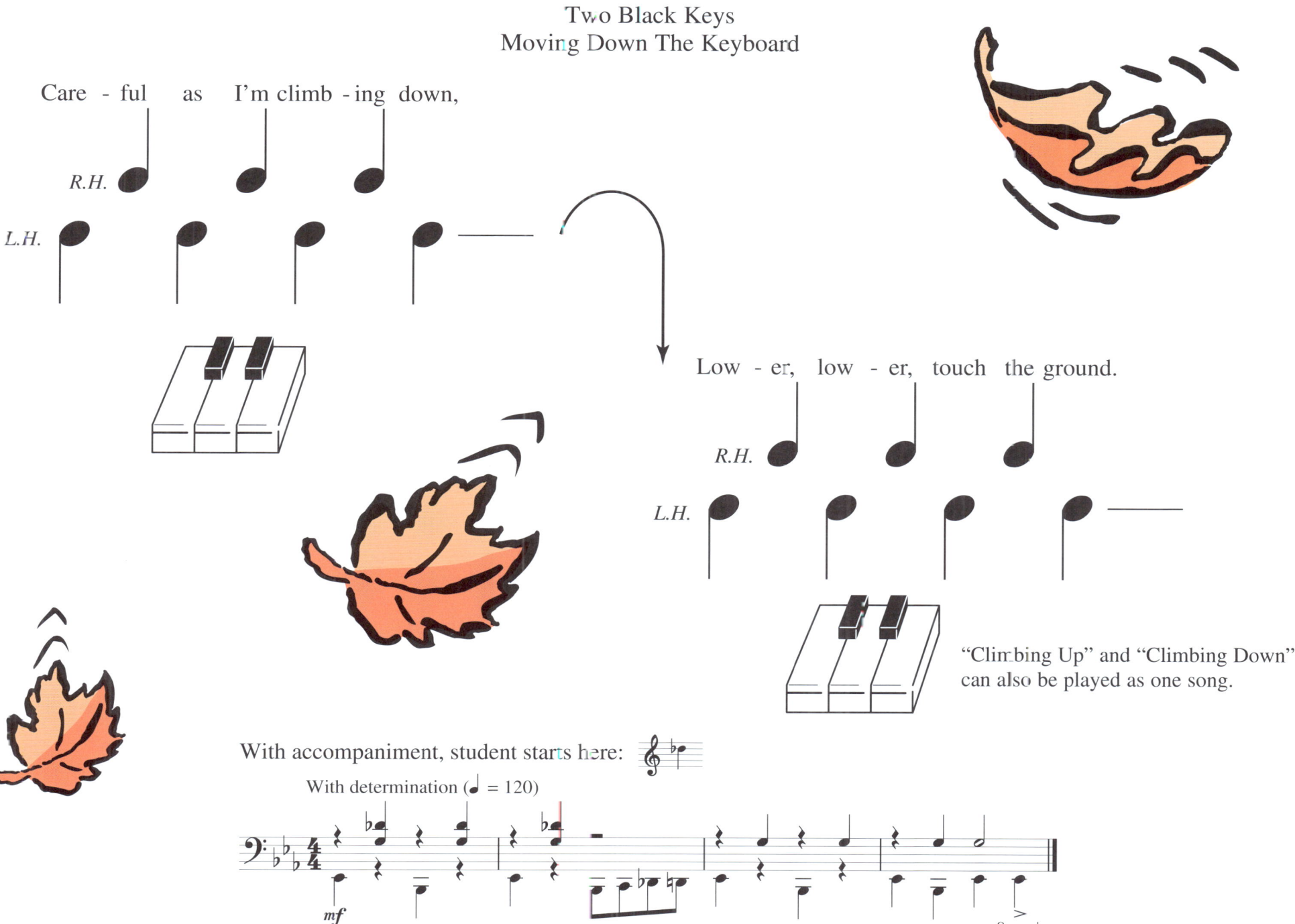

My Own Song

With your right and left hands, choose any groups of two black keys in the upper part of the piano.

Listen and feel the pulse as your teacher plays the accompaniment below. When you are ready, play along and make up your own song.

Have fun!

Accompaniment 🔊 8

Flowing (♩ = 100)

Repeat as necessary *Last time*

THREE BLACK KEYS

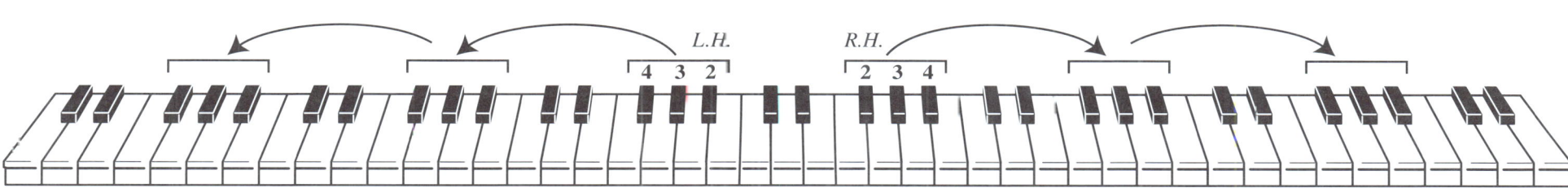

Low **High**

Using your **left hand**, start in the middle of the keyboard and play the groups of three black keys with fingers 2-3-4 going **down the keyboard**.

Using your **right hand**, start in the middle of the keyboard and play the groups of three black keys with fingers 2-3-4 going **up the keyboard**.

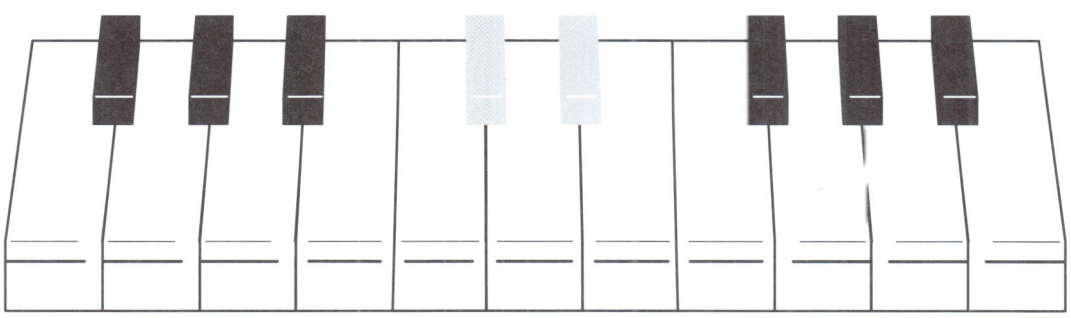

Play "My Own Song" again, using the groups of three black keys.

When you play these pieces by yourself, use the middle of the keyboard.

It is helpful to clap the rhythm of a piece before playing it.

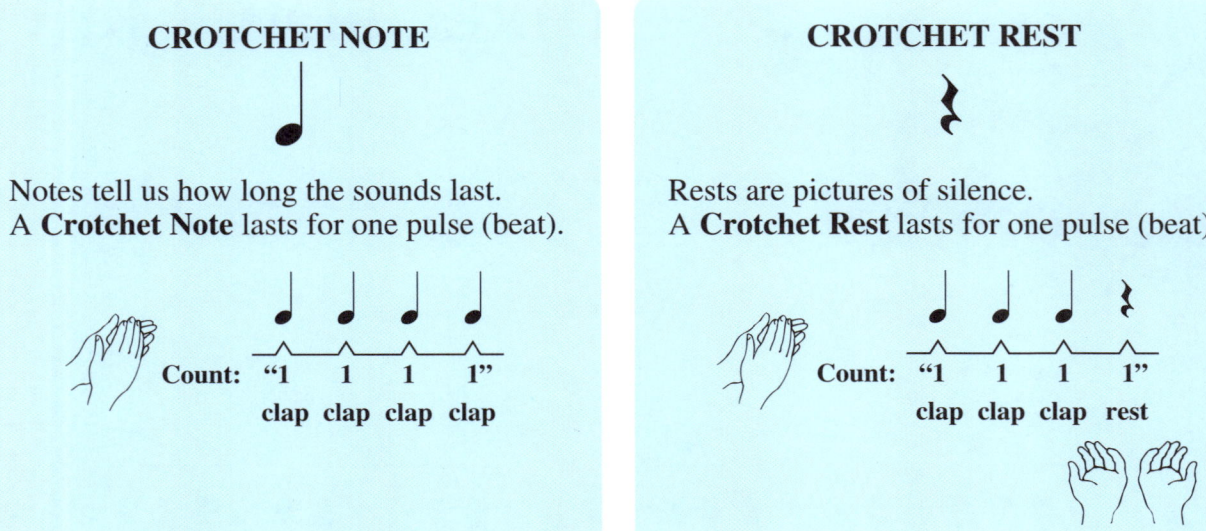

My Dog, Spike

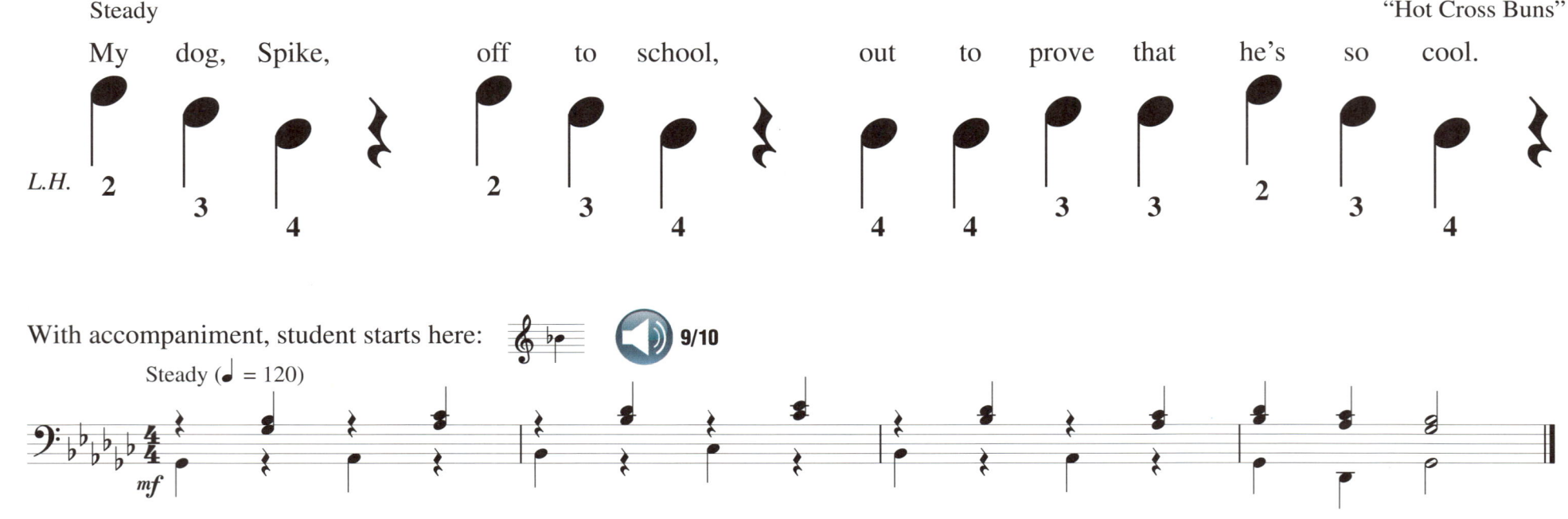

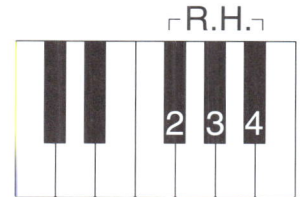

You can play "My Dog, Spike" and "Sorry, Spike" as one song.

Sorry, Spike

"Sor - ry, Spike! You won't pass! Bark - ing is - n't taught in class!"

With accompaniment, student starts here:

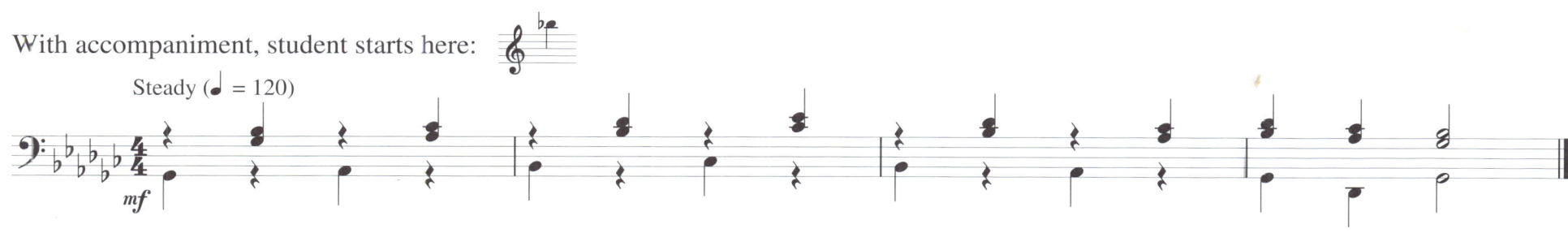

Party Cat's Bubbles

Party Cat loves to make bubbles.
Trace and colour each one.

Notes

Notes are pictures of sound.

Turn Party Cat's bubbles into notes.
Trace and colour each one.

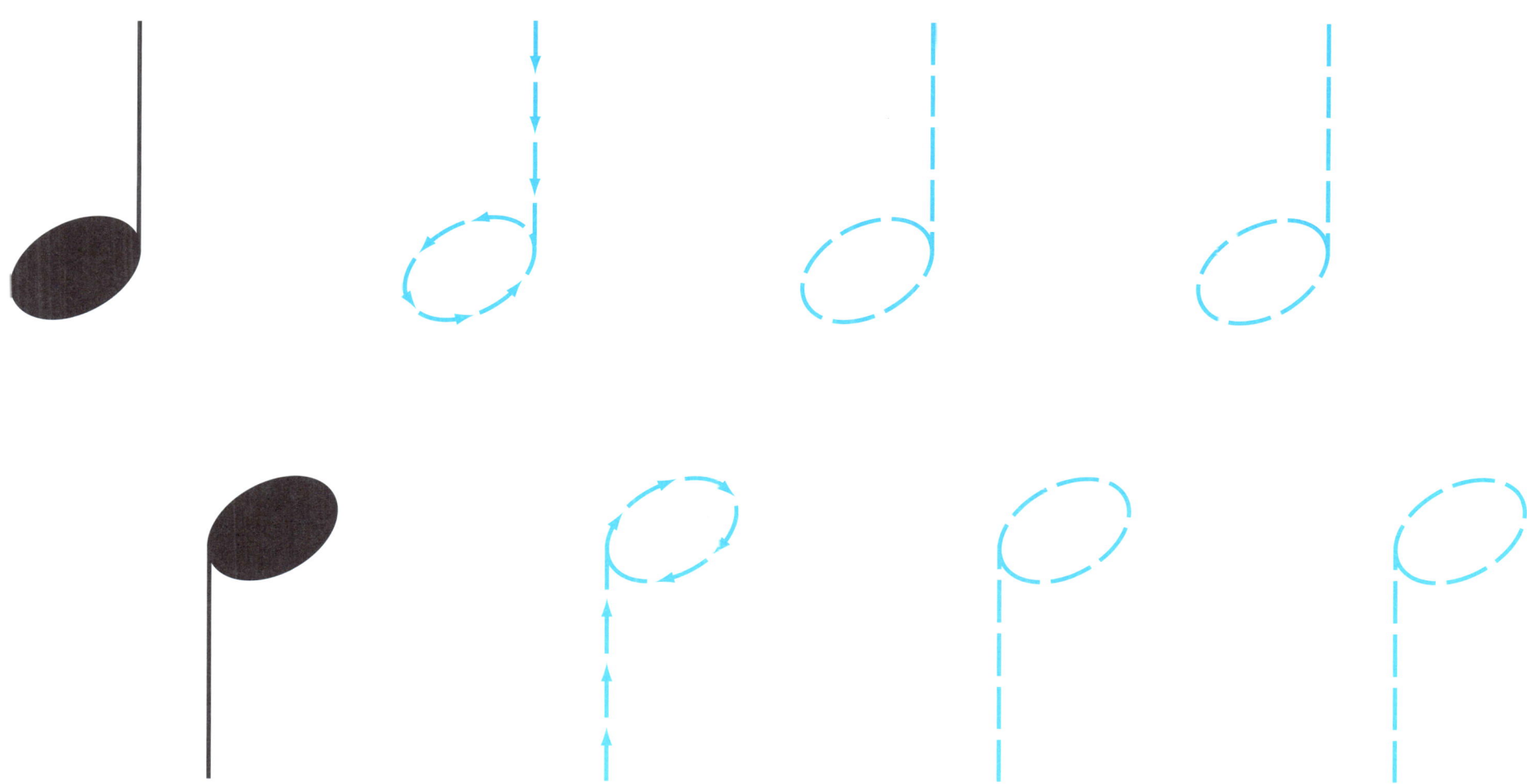

Listen & Respond

🔊 9

My Dog, Spike
(Activity Page)

1. As you listen to *My Dog, Spike*, clap and count the following rhythm two times:

   ♩ ♩ ♩ 𝄽 ♩ ♩ ♩ 𝄽 ♩ ♩ ♩ ♩ ♩ ♩ ♩ 𝄽

2. Trace and colour the crotchet notes: Trace the crotchet rests:

3. Complete the rhythm for *My Dog, Spike* by drawing the pictures of sound (♩) and the pictures of silence (𝄽) in the boxes below. When you are finished, tap and count the rhythm you wrote.

My	dog,	Spike,		off	to	school,		out	to	prove	that	he's	so	cool.
♩	♩	♩	𝄽				𝄽							𝄽

20

Left Hand

Left or Right?

Write "L.H." in the left hands and "R.H." in the right hands.

Right Hand

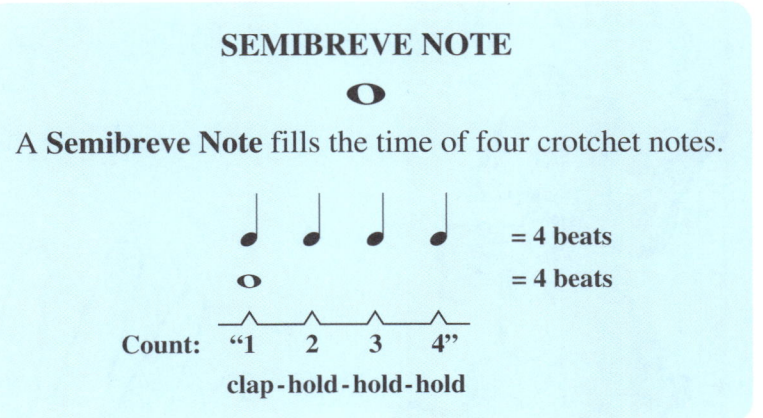

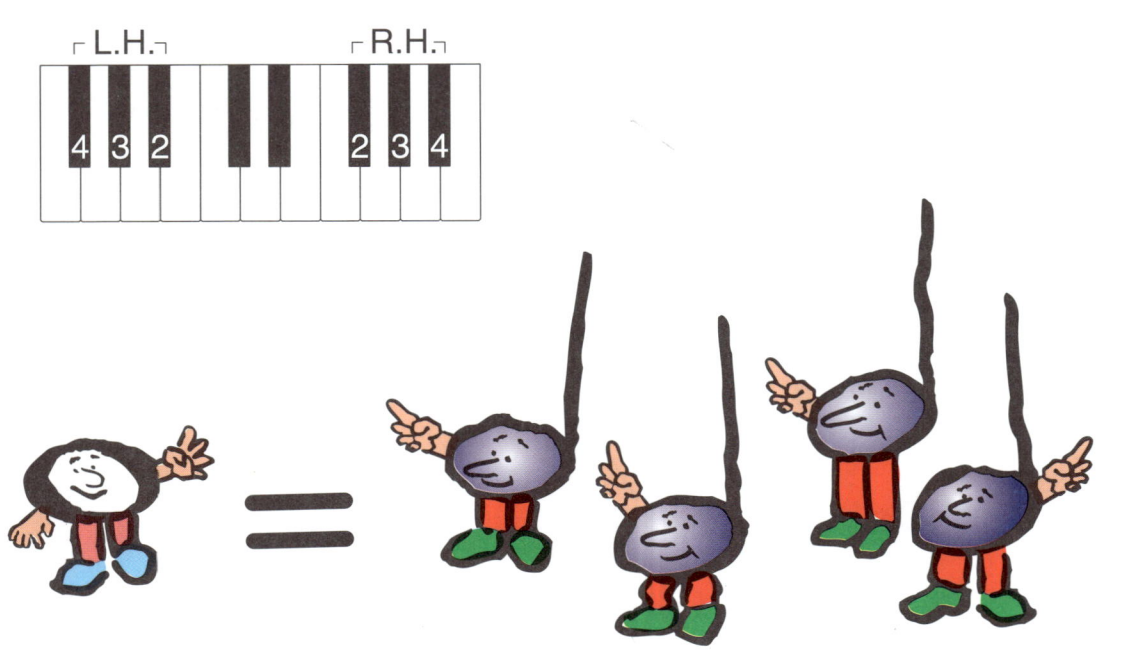

Merrily We're Off To School

Bouncy   "Mary Had A Little Lamb"

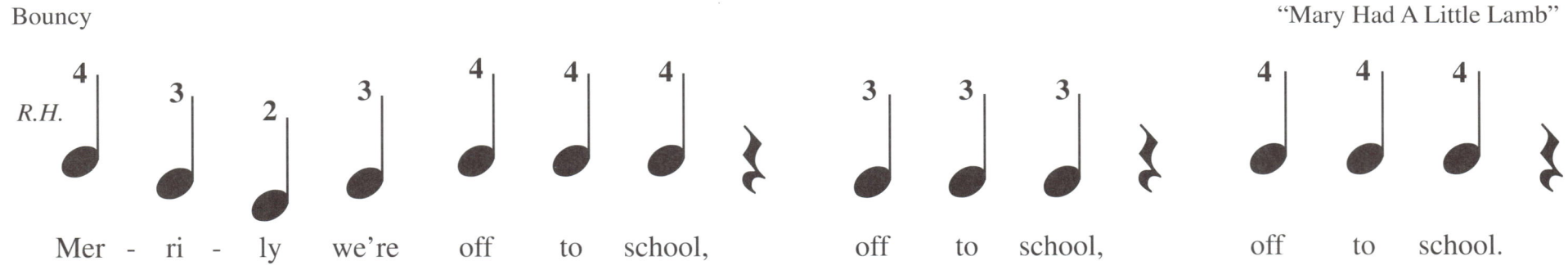

With accompaniment, student starts here: 🔊 11/12

■ *These small black boxes are called "clusters."*
Play notes together using fingers indicated.

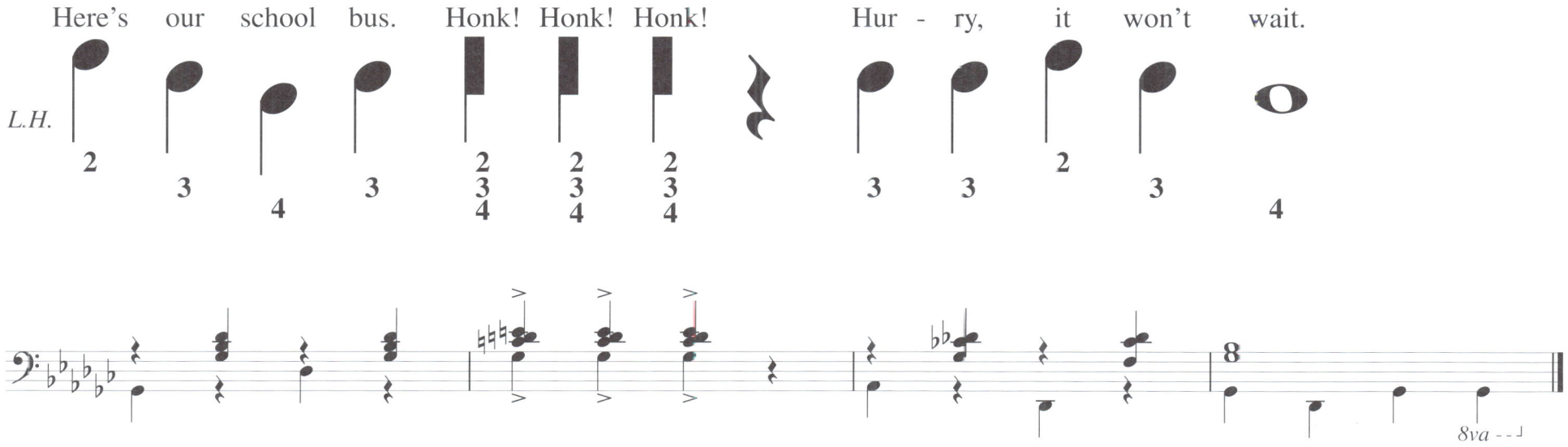

Listen & Respond

🔊 11

**Technique Tunes
by Katherine Glaser**

As you listen to *Merrily We're Off To School*, play this **Technique Tune**. Use energy from your whole arm, keeping your fingers close to the keys.

Merrily We're Off To School
(Activity Page)

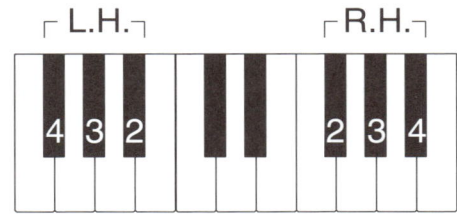

Repeat as necessary.

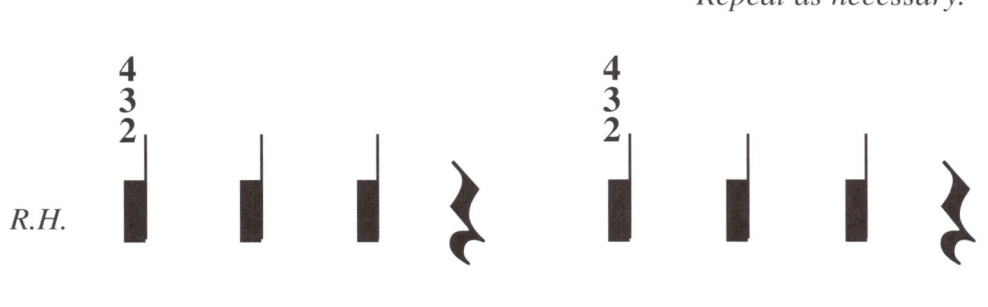

Honk! Honk! Honk!   Honk! Honk! Honk!

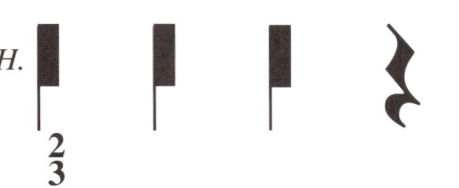 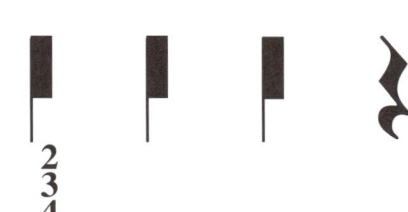

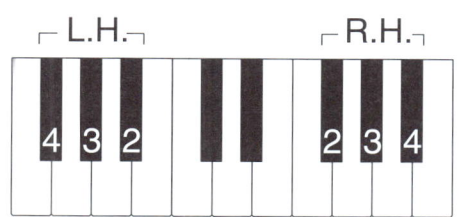

Long Shadows

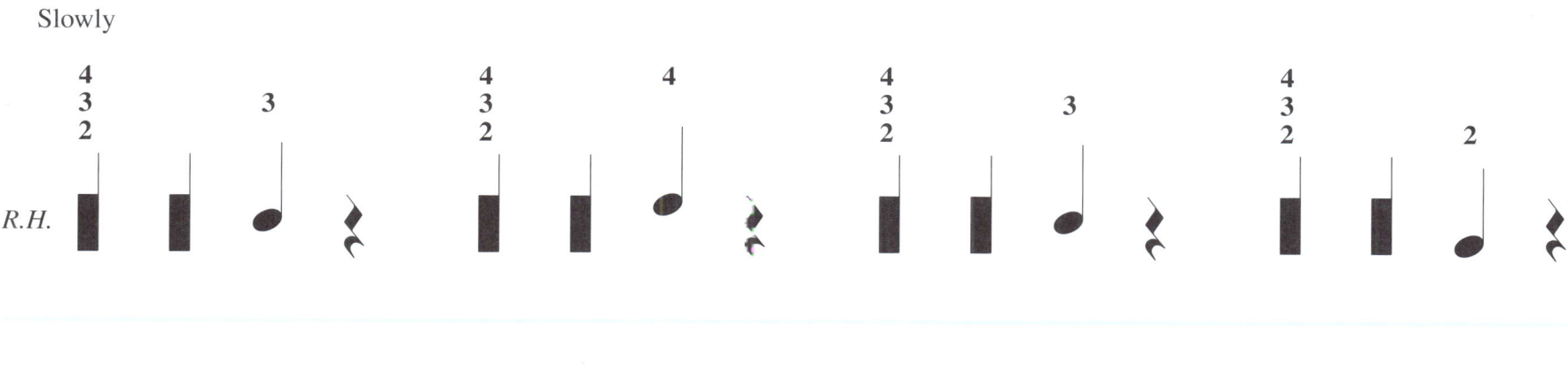

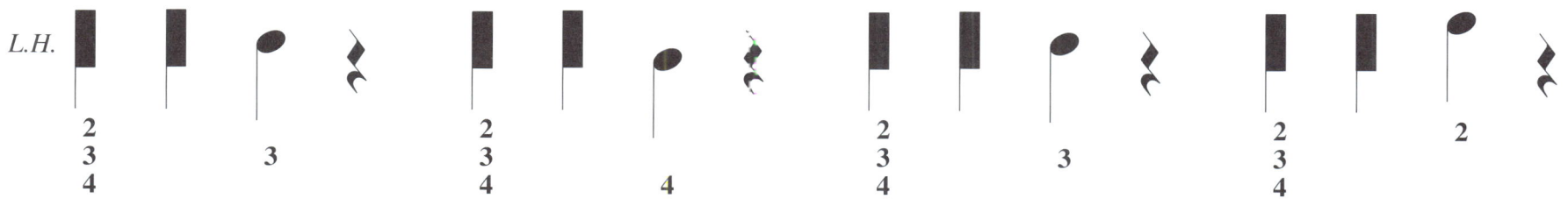

With accompaniment, student starts here:

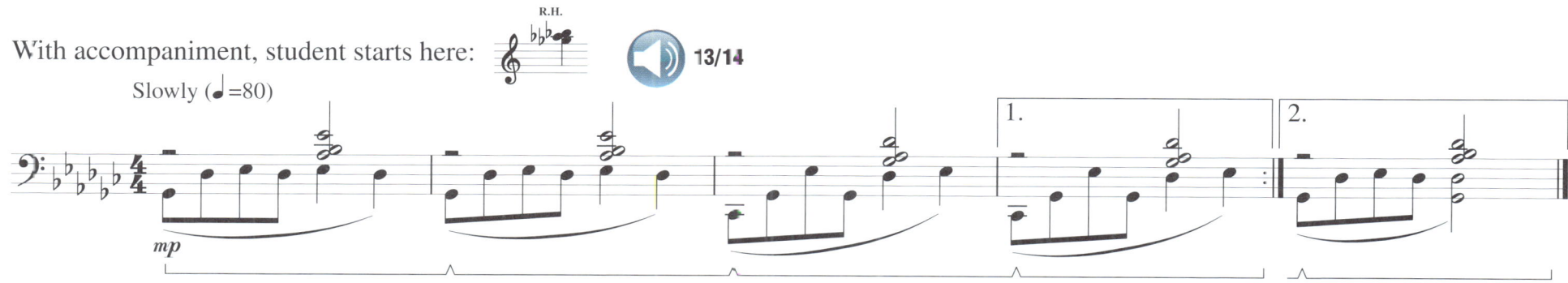

My Best Friend

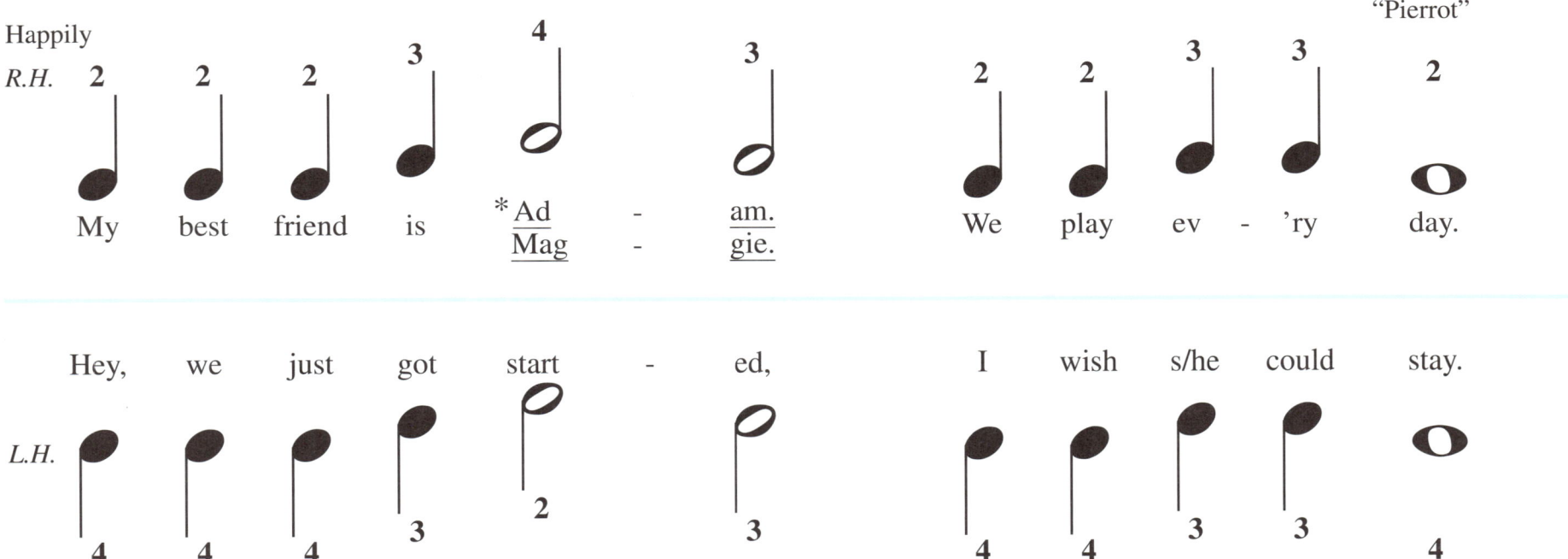

Play the first line of the song with your right hand; then play the second line of the song with your left hand.
*Fill in the name of your own friend.

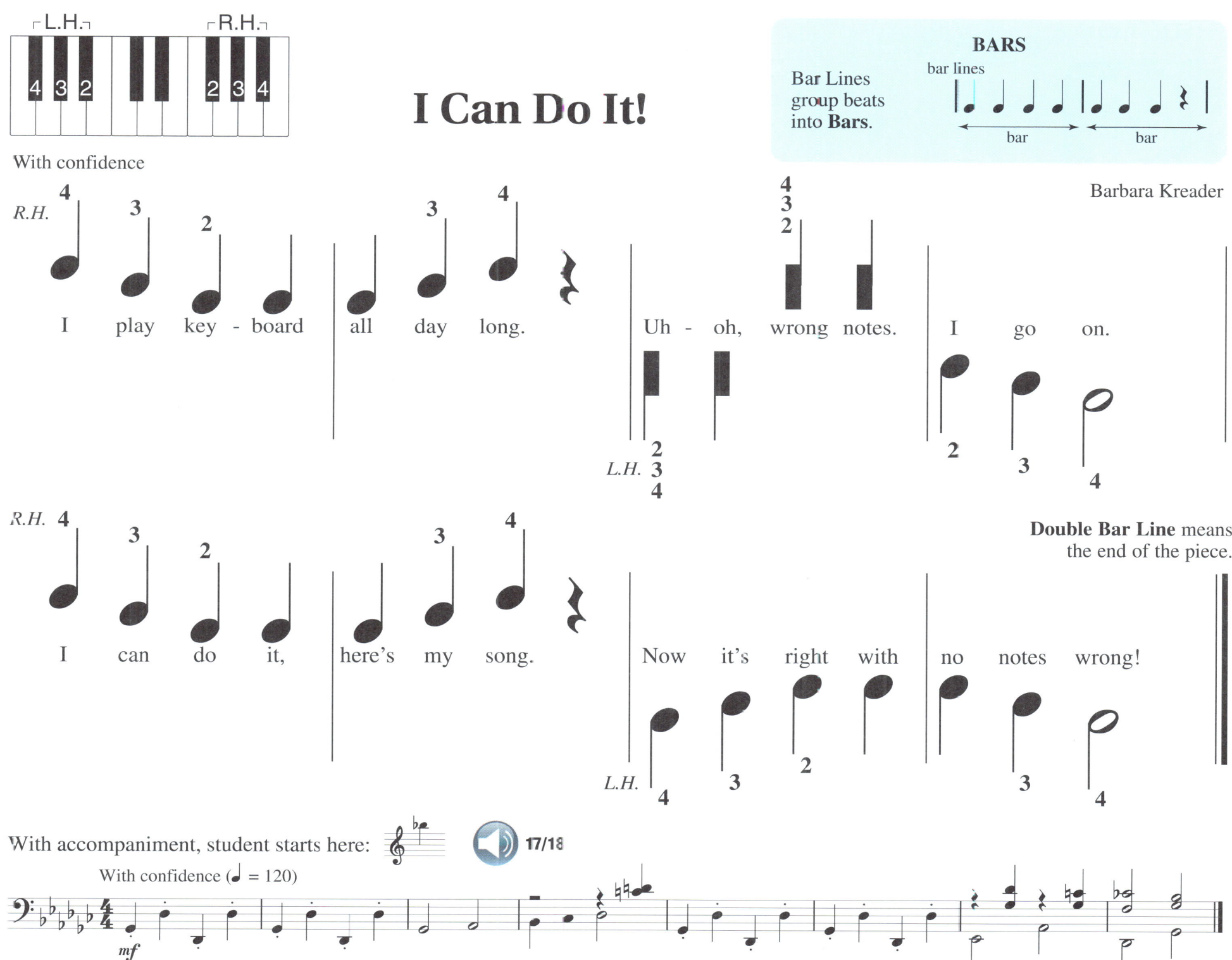

Read & Discover

I Can Do It!
(Activity Page)

Repeated Notes
Trace two repeated notes:

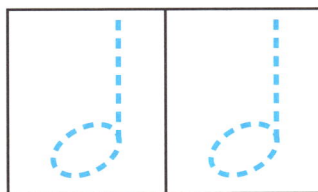

Stepping Down
Trace two notes stepping down:

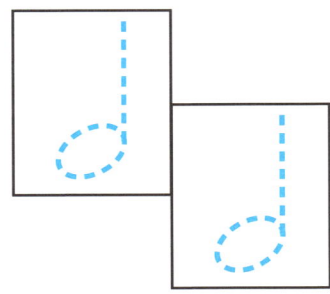

Stepping Up
Trace two notes stepping up:

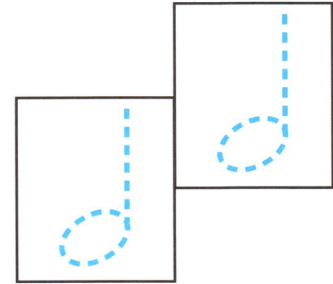

Complete this picture of *I Can Do It!*
1. Draw notes in the boxes and finger numbers in the blanks.
2. Play what you have written.

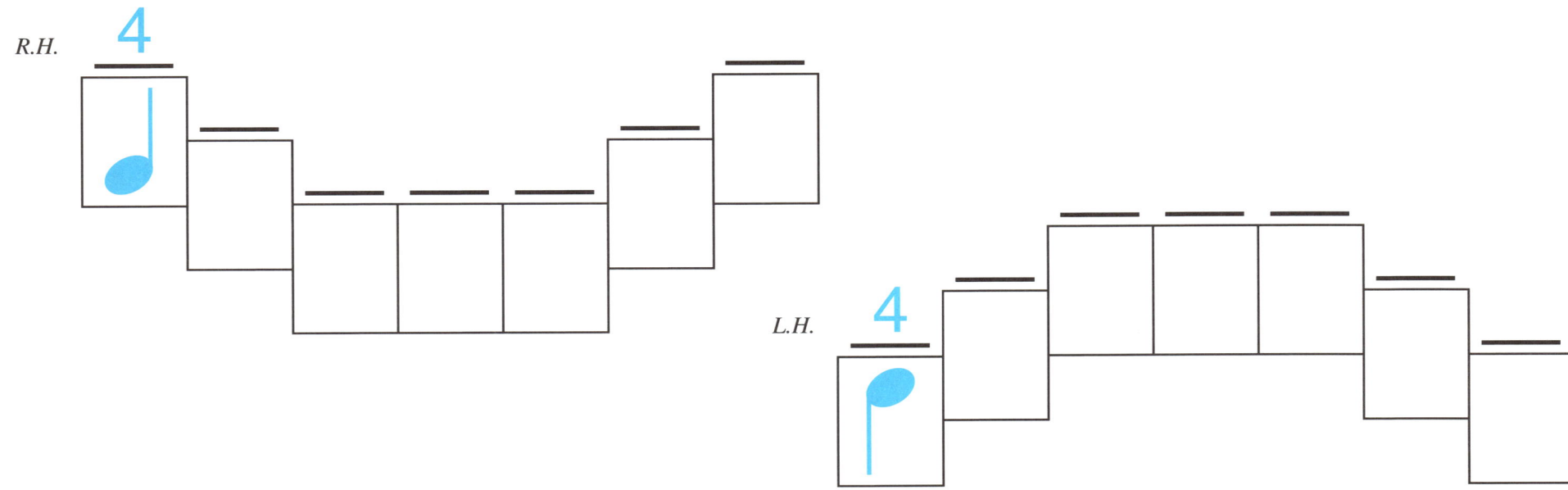

28

Which Hand Plays?

♩ Stems down = L.H.

♩ Stems up = R.H.

Circle the hand that plays each note.

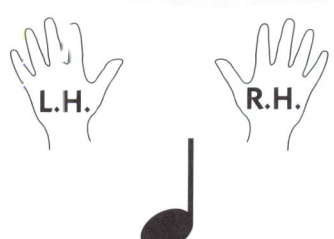

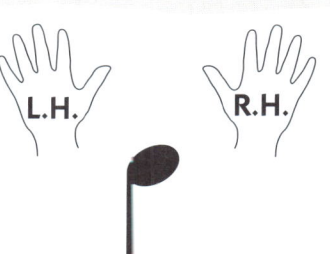

Draw the stem to match each hand.

L.H.   **R.H.**

L.H.   **R.H.**   **L.H.**

L.H.
R.H.
3 2
2 3 4

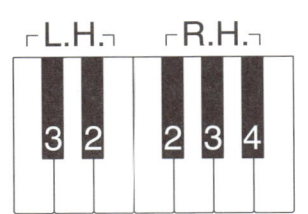

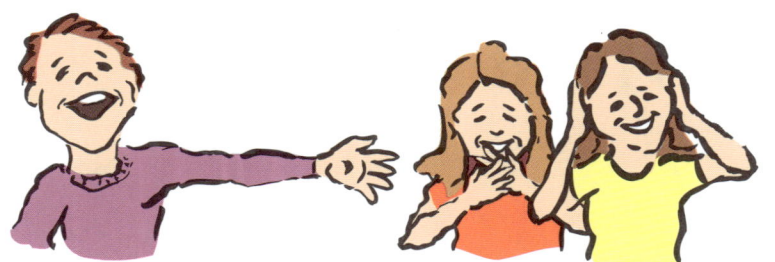

MINIM REST

A **Minim Rest** fills the time of two crotchet rests.

= 2 beats
= 2 beats

Count: "1 2"
rest - rest

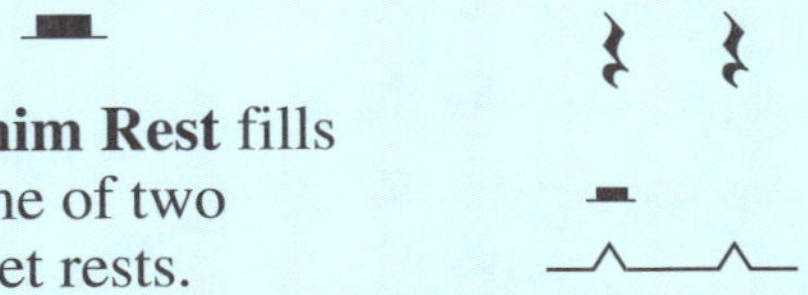

Let's Get Silly!

With excitement

Barbara Kreader

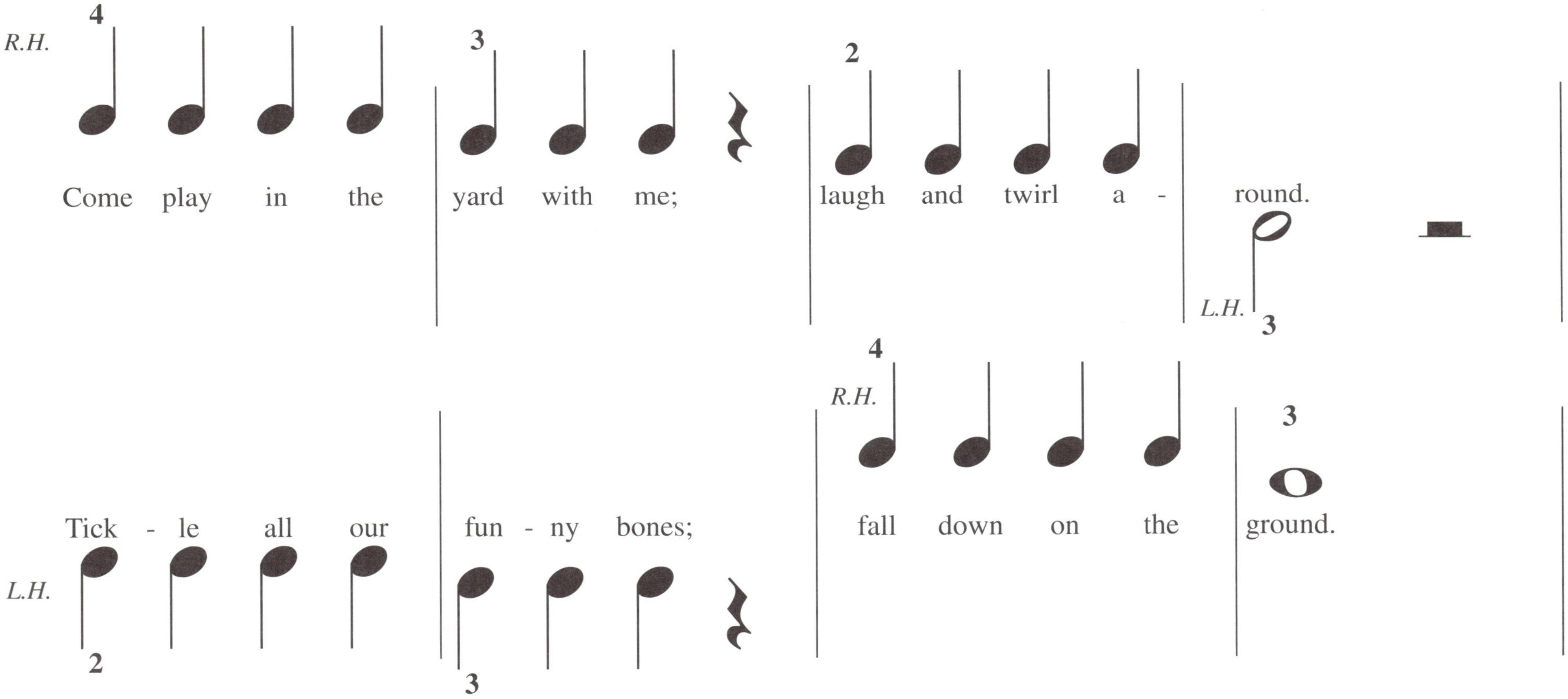

R.H.
4
Come play in the
3
yard with me;
2
laugh and twirl a - round.
L.H.
3
4
R.H.
Tick - le all our fun - ny bones; fall down on the ground.
L.H.
2
3
3

With accompaniment, student starts here: 19/20

With excitement
(♩ = 130)
mf
3
8va

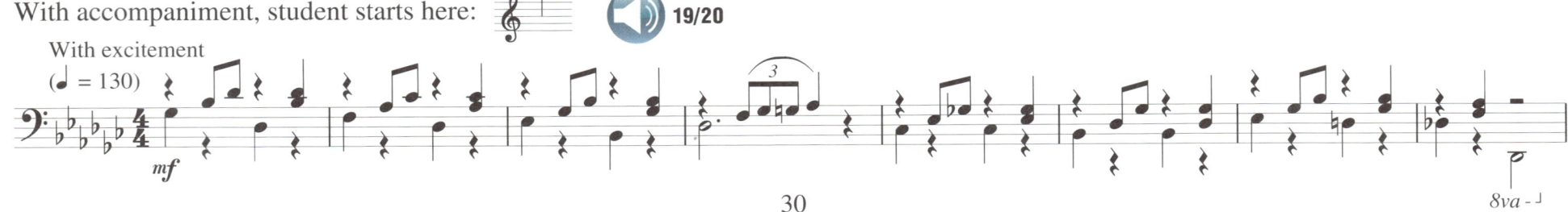

Drawing Rests

A rest is a picture of silence.

CROTCHET RESTS

Rest for one beat.

𝄽

I look like a squiggly line.

MINIM RESTS

Rest for two beats.

I look like a hat.

Trace these crotchet rests.

Trace these minim rests.

Your teacher will tap or play one of the rhythms in each box.
    1. Circle the rhythm you hear.
    2. Choose one note on the piano and play the rhythm you circled.

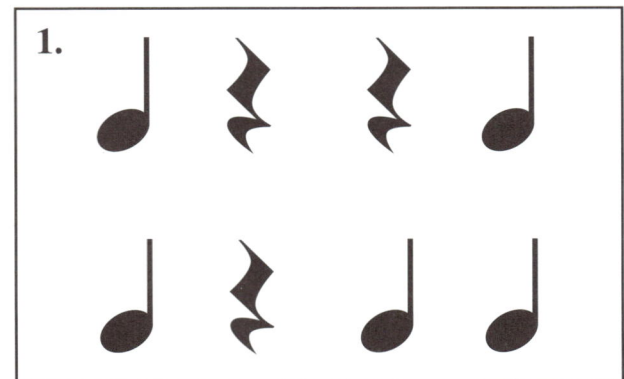 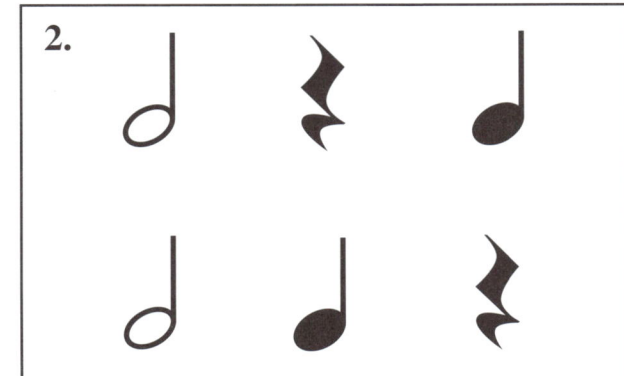 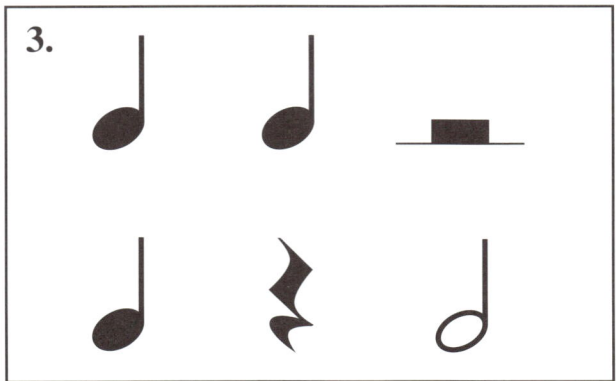

Rhythm Detective

Find the missing notes and rests!

A note or rest is missing from every bar below. When completed, every bar has exactly four beats.
1. Choose a correct note or rest from the detective's hat.
2. Draw the missing note or rest in the box in each bar.

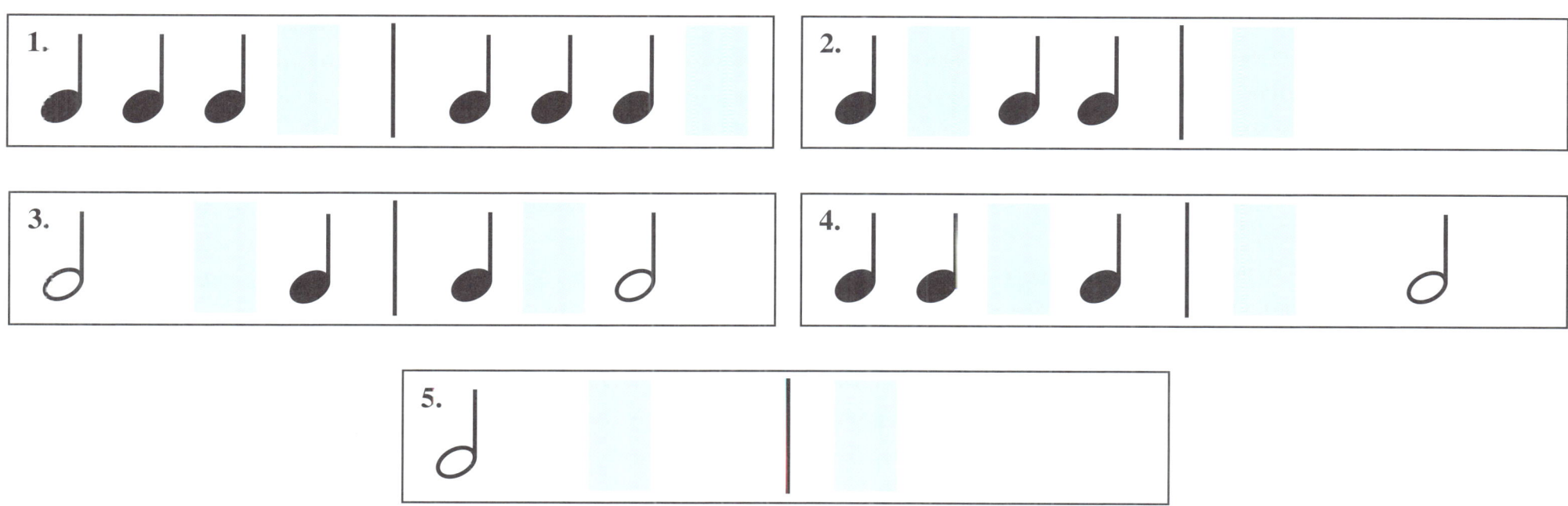

Now it's your teacher's turn to guess!
Choose a note on the piano and play one of the five rhythms keeping a steady pulse.
Ask your teacher to guess which rhythm you played.

L.H.
R.H.
3 2 2 3 4

Water Lily

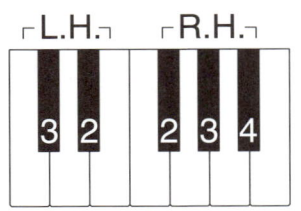

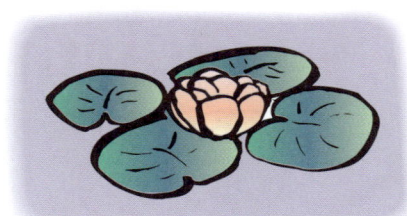

Delicately

Phillip Keveren

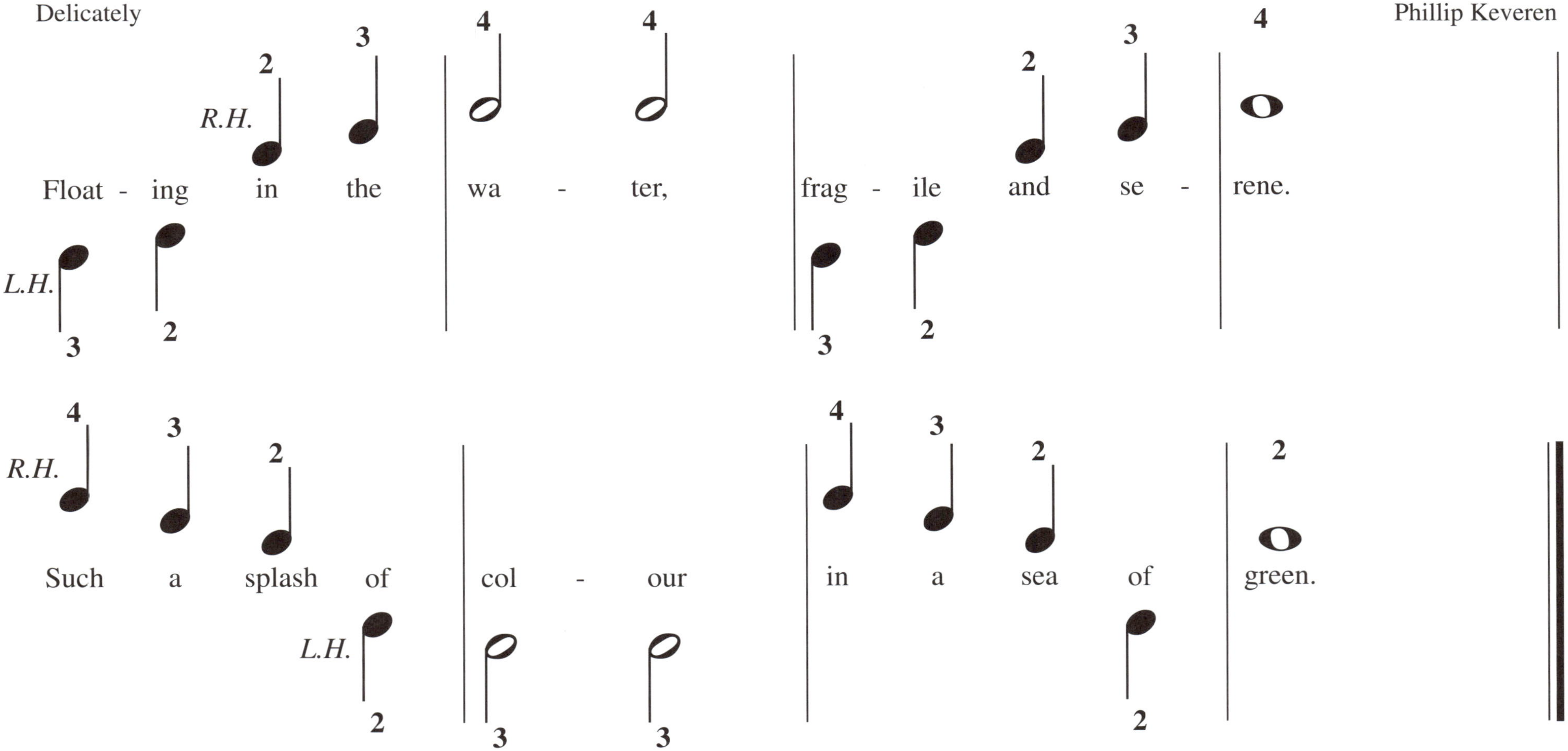

R.H.
L.H.
Float - ing in the wa - ter, frag - ile and se - rene.
Such a splash of col - our in a sea of green.

With accompaniment, student starts here: 21/22

Delicately (♩ = 95)

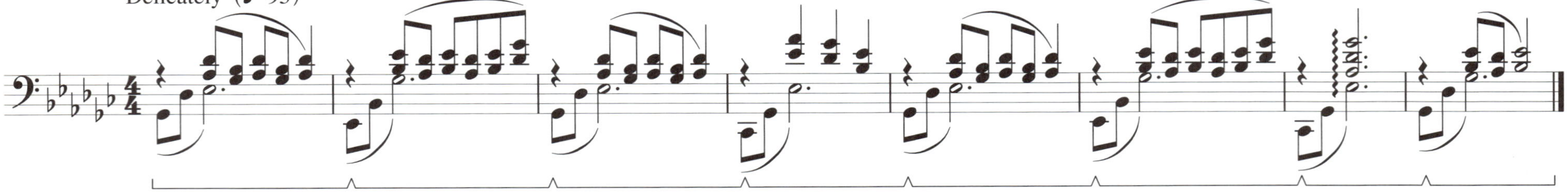

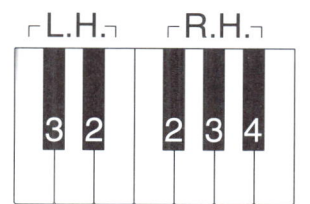

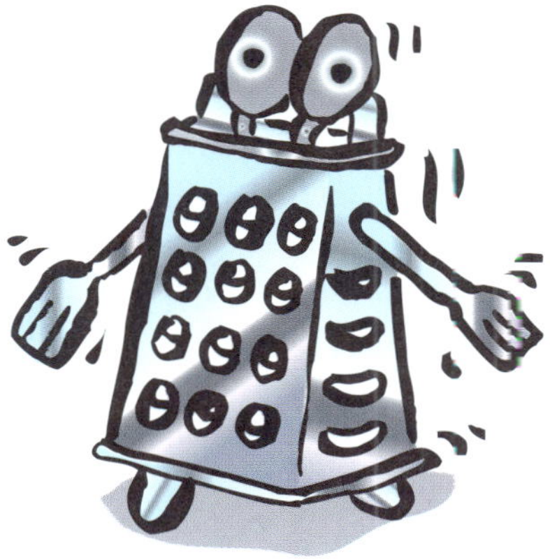

Mister Machine

Deliberately

Bill Boyd

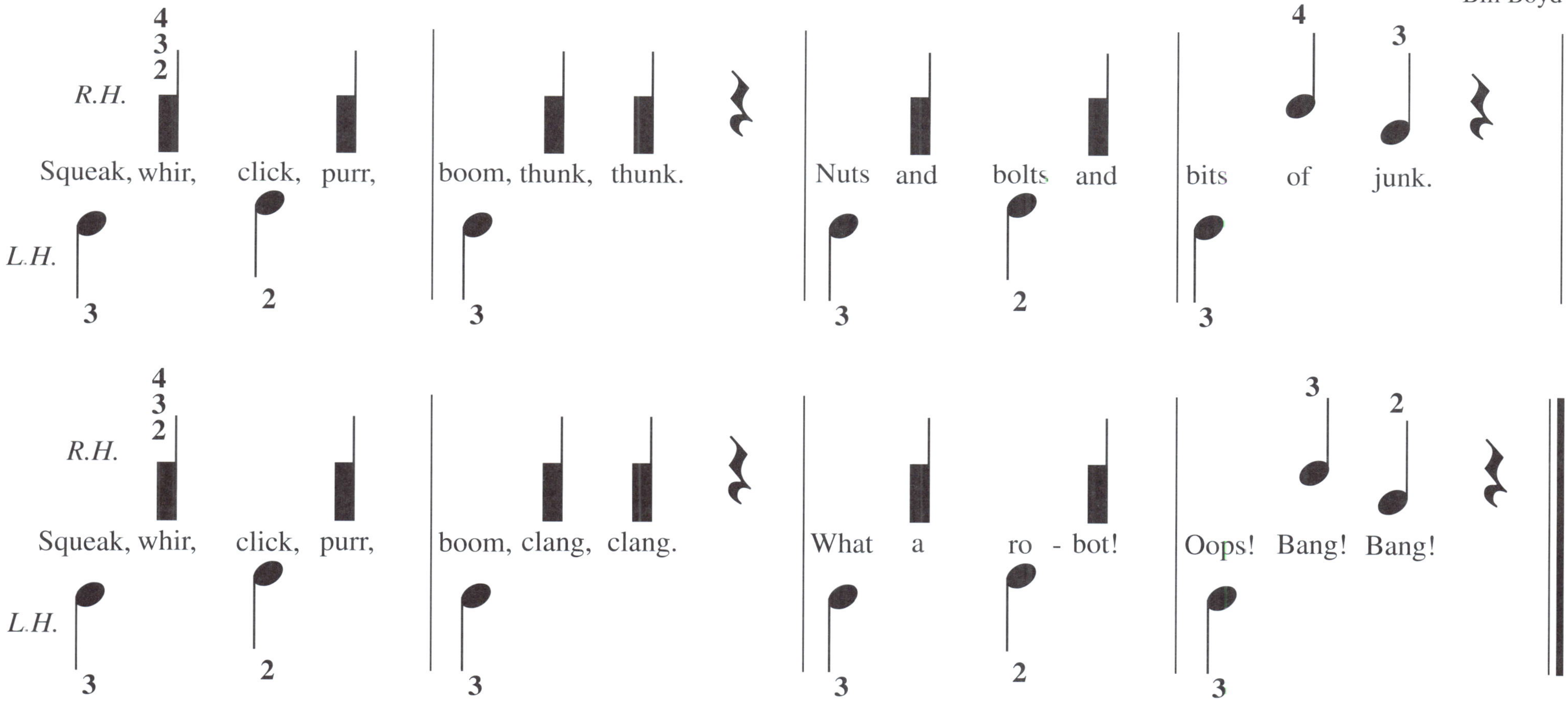

R.H.
4
3
2

Squeak, whir, click, purr, boom, thunk, thunk. Nuts and bolts and bits of junk.

L.H.
3 2 3 3 2 3

R.H.
4
3
2

Squeak, whir, click, purr, boom, clang, clang. What a ro - bot! Oops! Bang! Bang!

L.H.
3 2 3 3 2 3

With accompaniment, student starts here:
Deliberately (♩= 130)   23/24

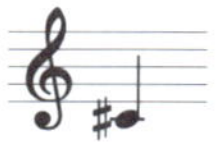

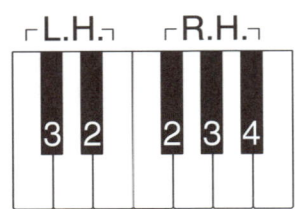

Walking The Dog

Lazy   Fred Kern

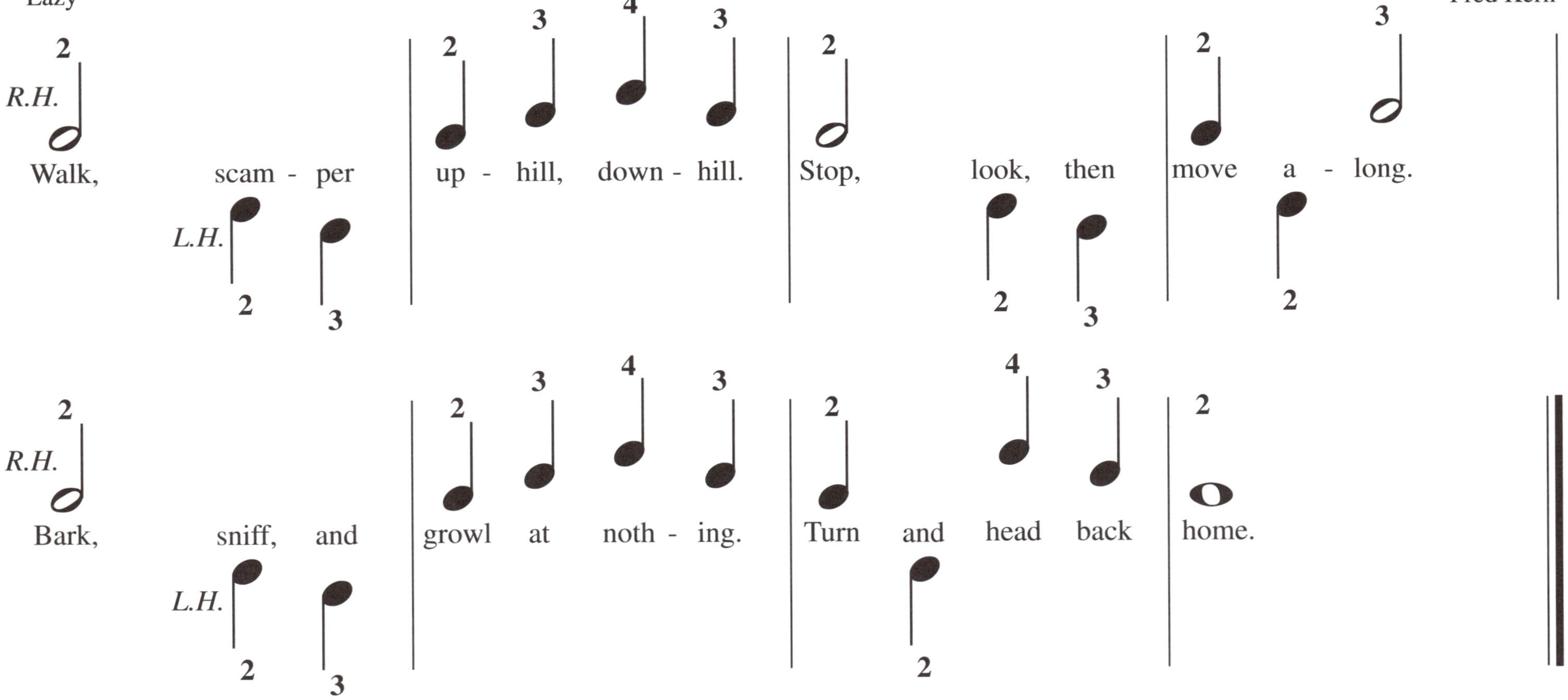

R.H. Walk, scamper up-hill, down-hill. Stop, look, then move a-long.

L.H.

R.H. Bark, sniff, and growl at noth-ing. Turn and head back home.

With accompaniment, student starts here: 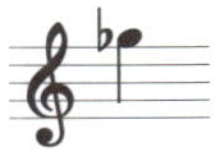 🔊 25/26

Lazy (♪♪ = ♪♩) (♩ = 105)

36

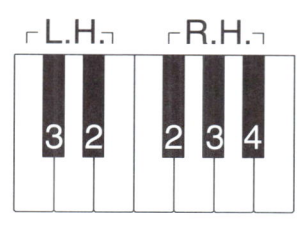

Night Shadows

Quietly

Barbara Kreader

Shad - ows, shad - ows on the wall. My bear is scared and so am I.

But my night light's shin - ing. We can go to sleep.

With accompaniment, student starts here: 🔊 27/28

Quietly (♩ = 82)

p

With pedal

37

Listen & Respond

 27

Night Shadows
(Activity Page)

As you listen to *Night Shadows*, tap and count the following rhythm. Remember, ♩ = R.H. ↑ = L.H.

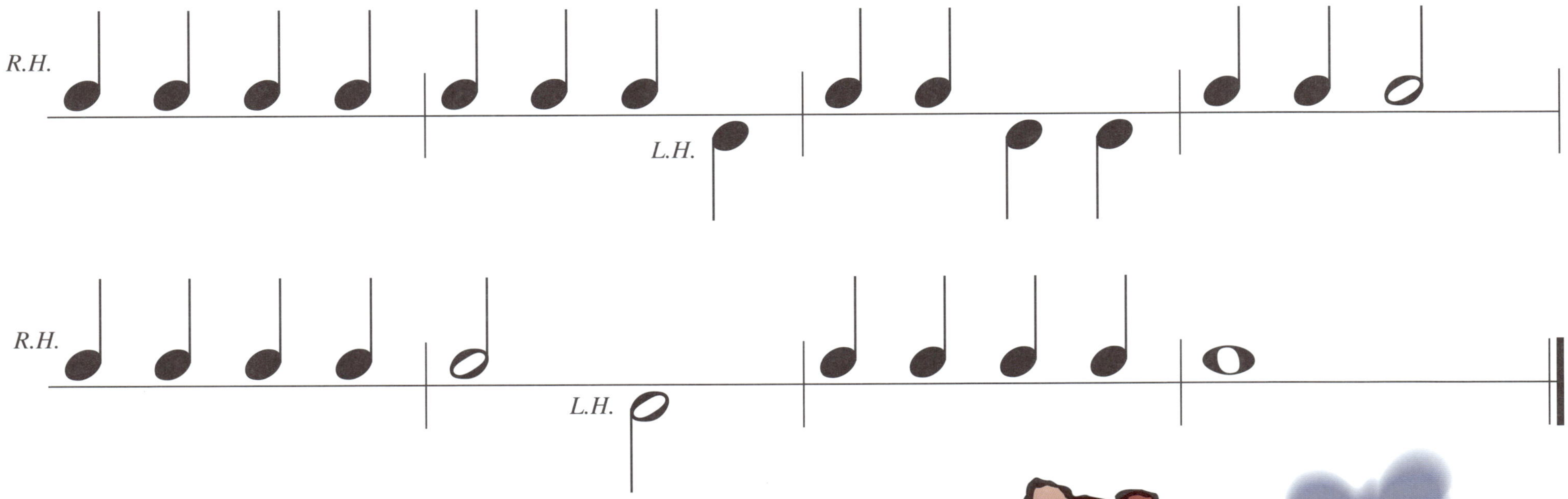

Rhythm Composer

Each fish bowl contains the notes and rests you will need to compose the bars below.

1-beat fish bowl

4-beat fish bowl

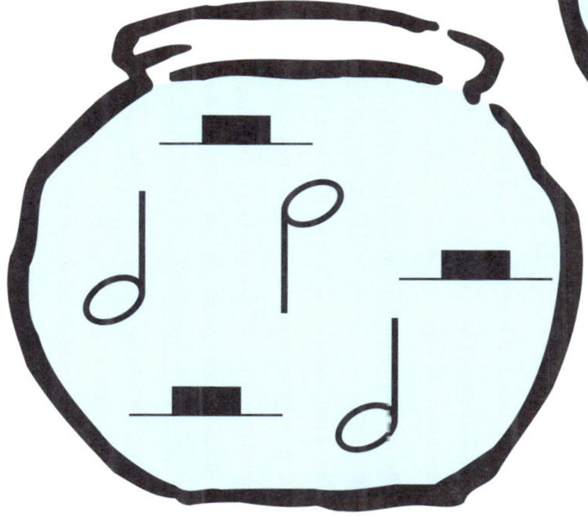

2-beat fish bowl

double bar
repeat sign
(means to play the piece again)

Each bar needs exactly four beats.
Choose notes or rests from each fish bowl and draw them in the bars below.

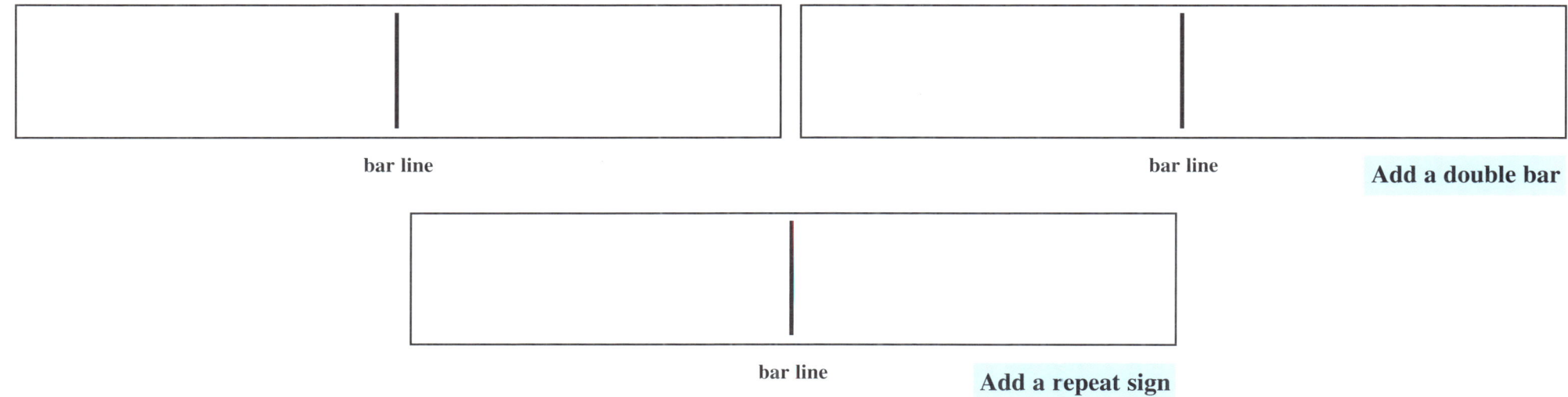

bar line

bar line

Add a double bar

bar line

Add a repeat sign

39

THE MUSICAL ALPHABET

Playing on the White Keys

Music uses the first seven letters of the alphabet. These letters are used over and over to name the white keys.

Alphabet Soup

With your right-hand third finger, play and sing the music alphabet three times, using this rhythm:

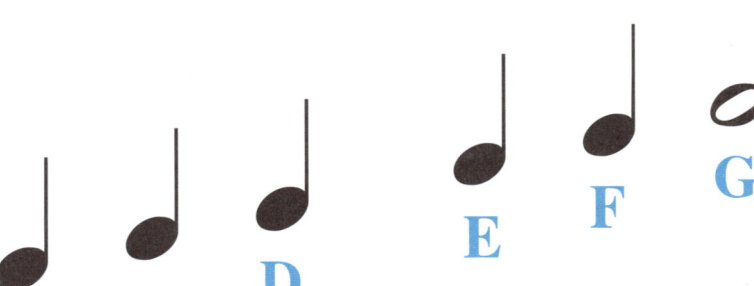

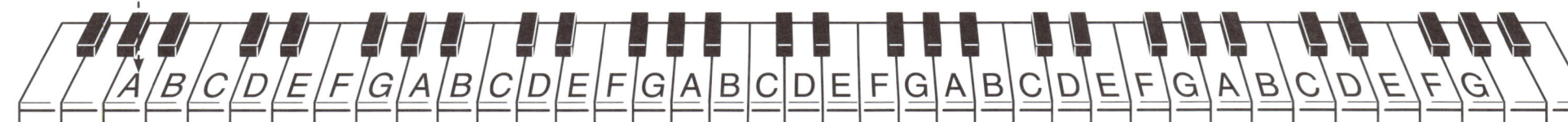

Student part to be played by rote. 🔊 29

Fred Kern

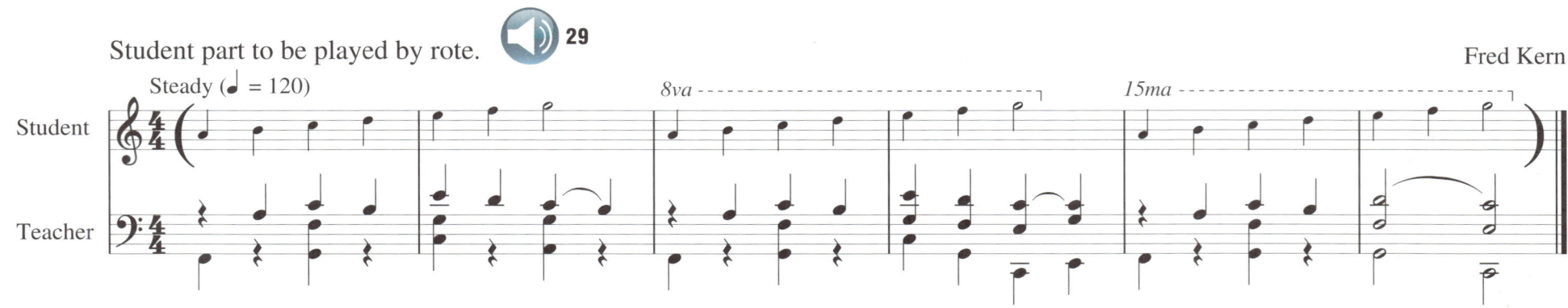

40

The Musical Alphabet

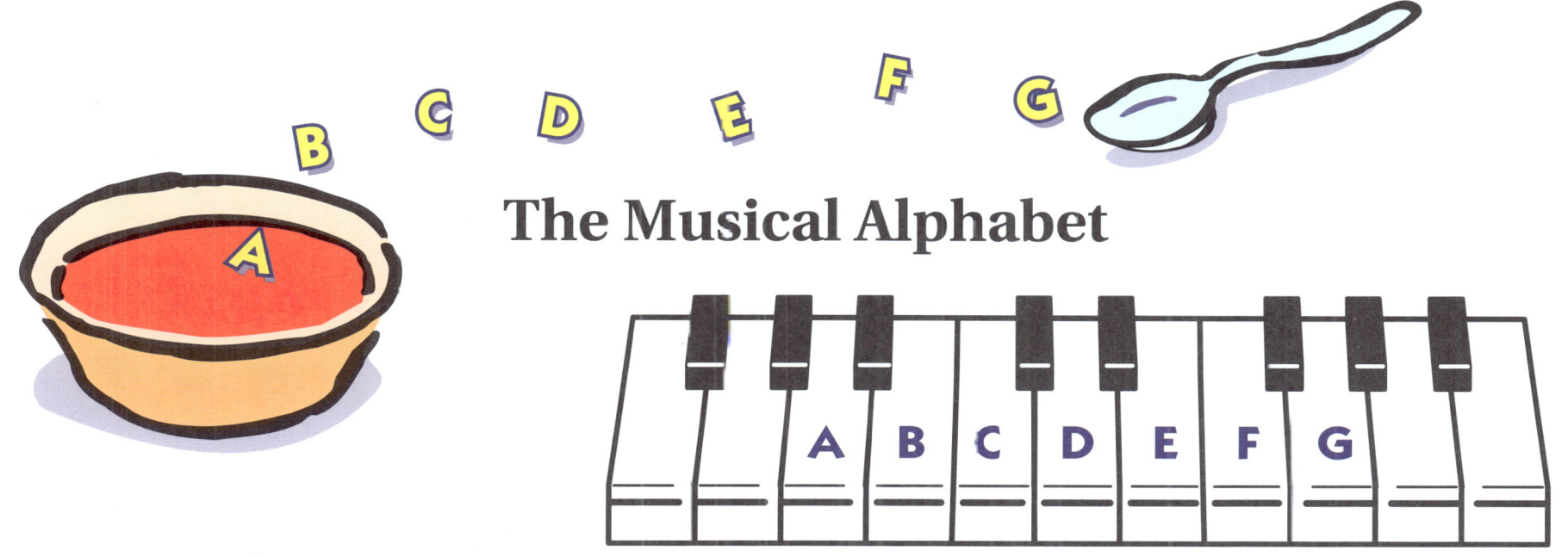

On each keyboard below, start with the given letter and write the musical alphabet. The arrows will direct you to write the alphabet forwards or backwards.

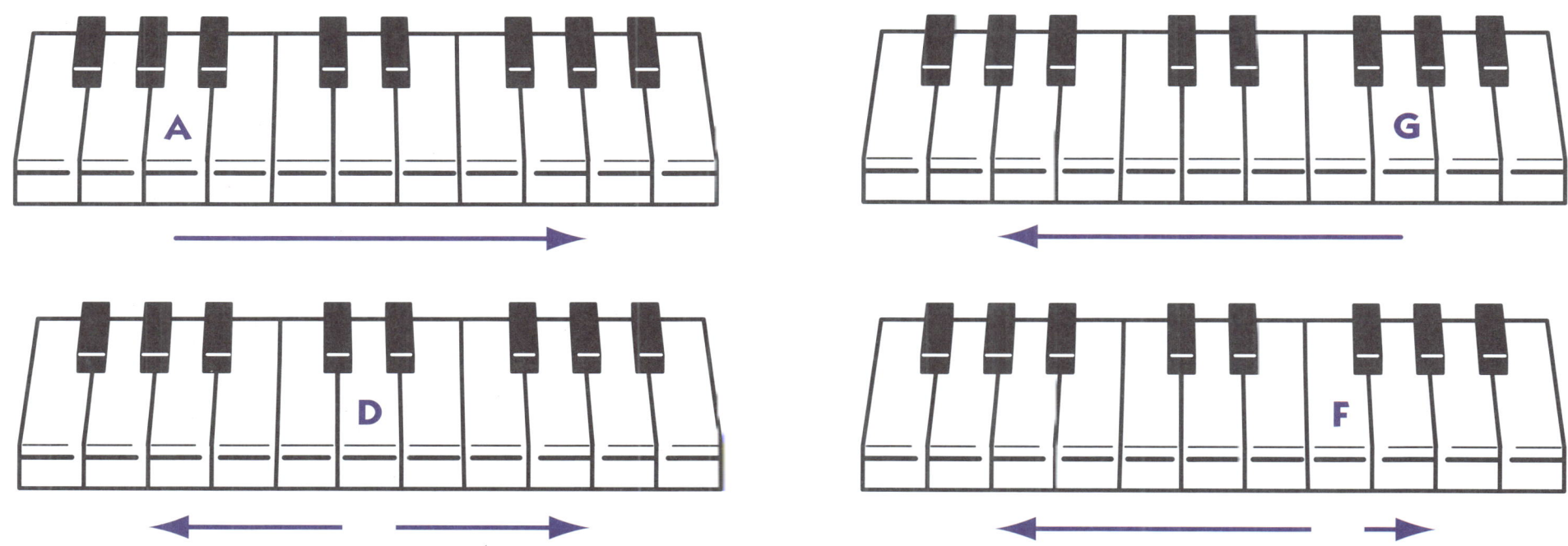

The Attic Stairs

Sing the musical alphabet forward and backward as you play "The Attic Stairs." Keep your thumb behind the first joint of your third finger.

Climb the stairs **two** times. Use finger 3.
1. R.H. alone.
2. L.H. alone.

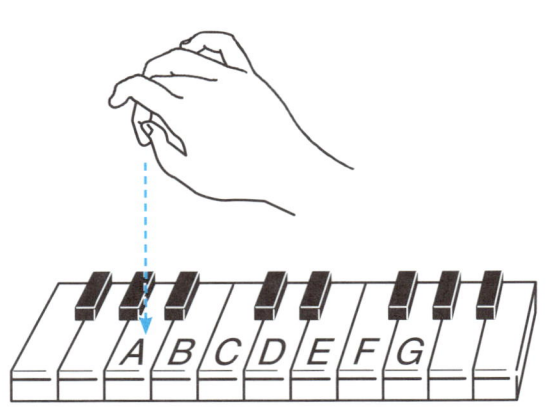

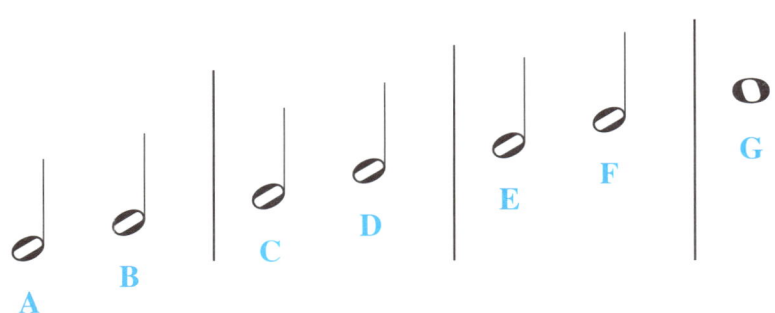

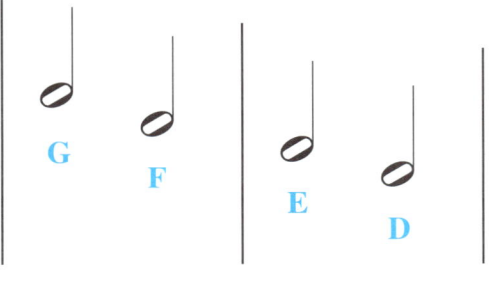

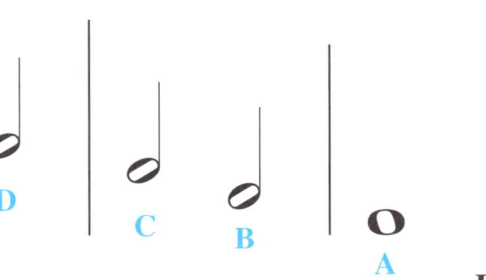

Repeat Sign means to play the piece again.

With accompaniment, student starts here:  30/31

Slowly (♩=100)

mp

42

C D E GROUPS

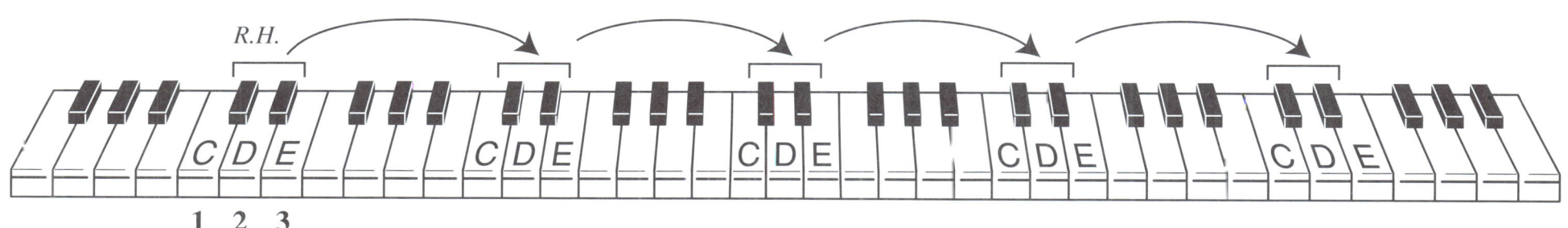

With your right hand, start at the low end of the keyboard and play the C D E groups with individual fingers 1-2-3 going up the keyboard.

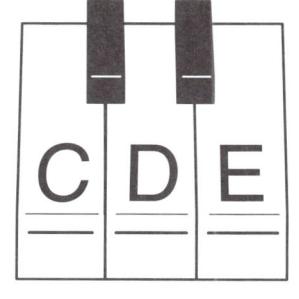

Now explore the keyboard, playing the C D E groups with your left hand using fingers 3-2-1.

C D E Groups
(Activity Page)

1. Circle the sets of two black keys.
2. Write the C D E letter names on the white keys.
3. Colour the C's red, the D's blue, and the E's green.

My Own Song On C D E

With your right or left hand, choose any C D E group in the upper part of the piano.

Listen and feel the pulse as your teacher plays the accompaniment below. When you are ready, play C D E. Experiment by playing E D C.

Mix the letters any way you want and make up your own song.

Have fun!

Accompaniment 🔊 32

Finding C D E on the Keyboard

Party Cat is inviting some animal friends to his birthday party, but he can't remember how to spell all their names.

Help him by filling in the missing letters.
1. Write the name of each outlined key in the blank below it.
2. Colour the C's red, the D's blue, and the E's green.

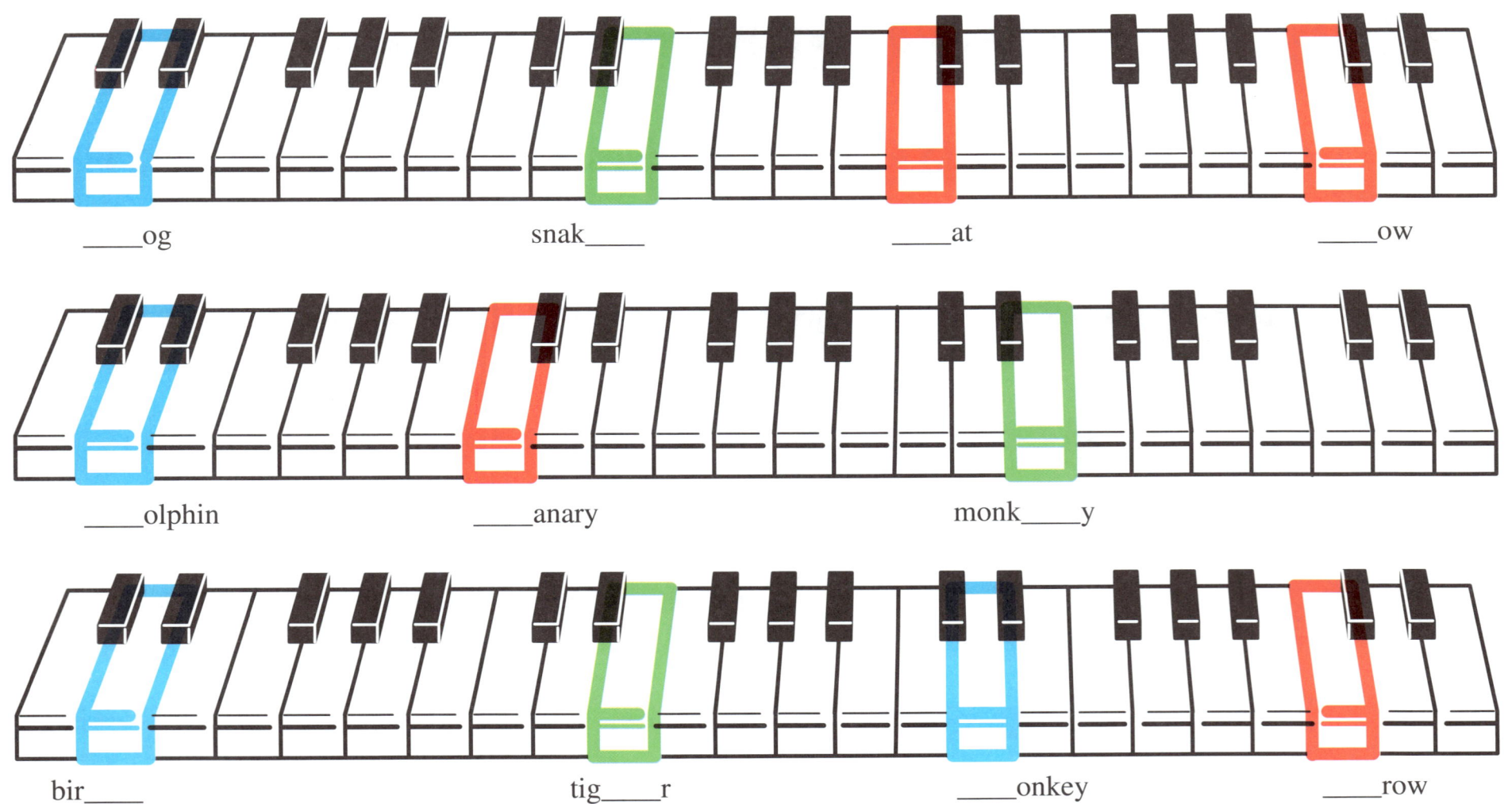

____og   snak____   ____at   ____ow

____olphin   ____anary   monk____y

bir____   tig____r   ____onkey   ____row

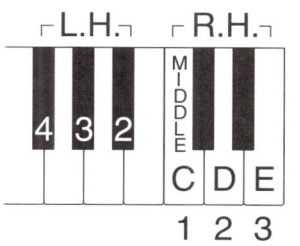

PIANO

p

means soft

Dynamic Signs tell how loud or soft to play and help create the mood of the music.

Balloon Ride

Phillip Keveren

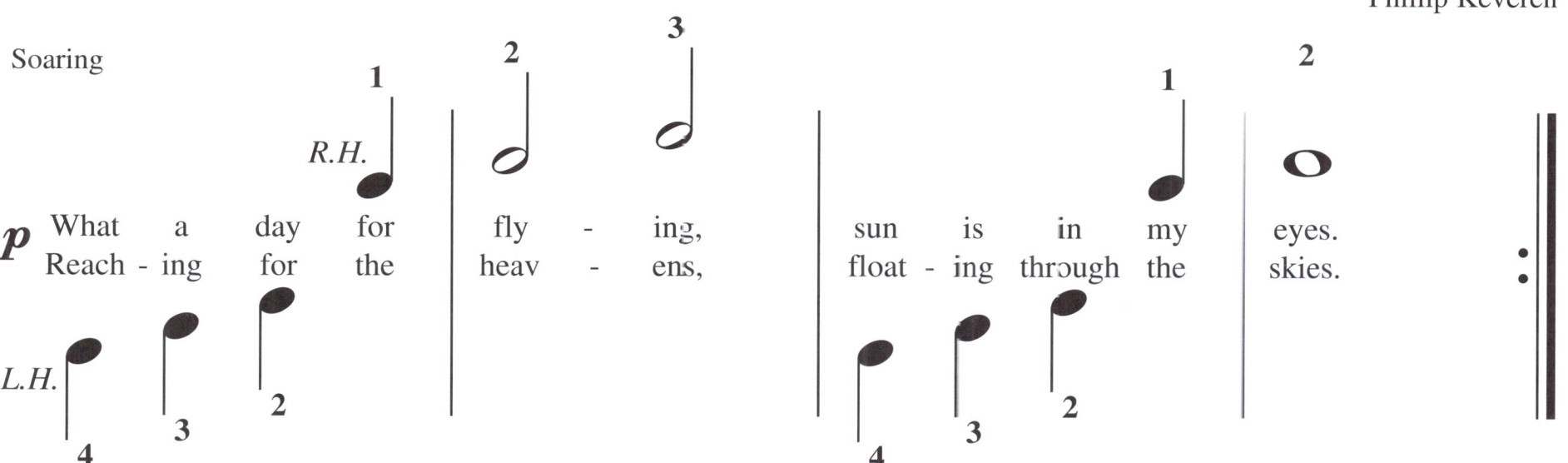

Soaring

p What a day for fly - ing, sun is in my eyes.
Reach - ing for the heav - ens, float - ing through the skies.

Hold down the right pedal (sustain pedal) throughout.

With accompaniment, student starts here: 🔊 33/34

Soaring (♩ = 120)

47

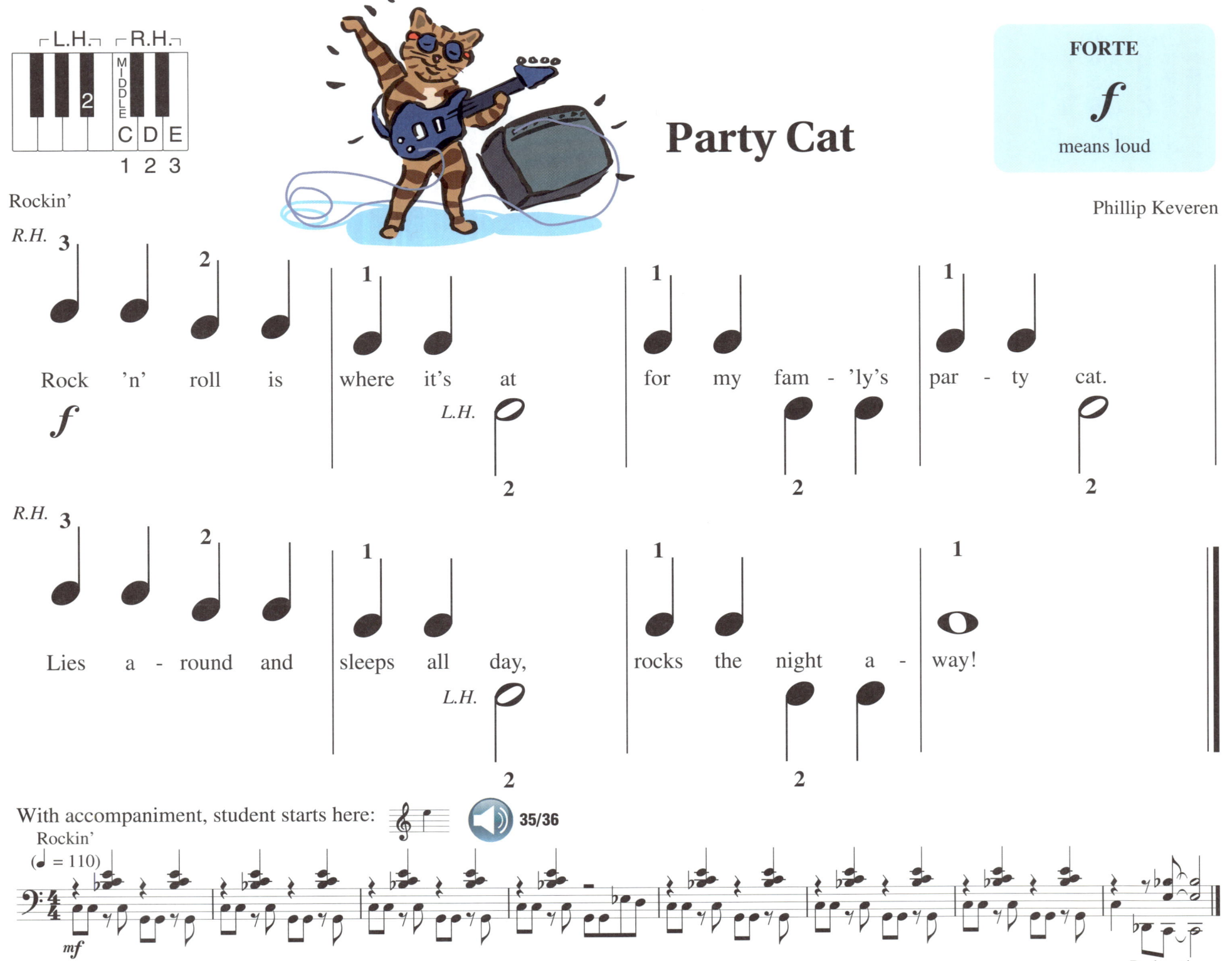

Imagine & Create

Write in the C D E groups on the keyboard below.

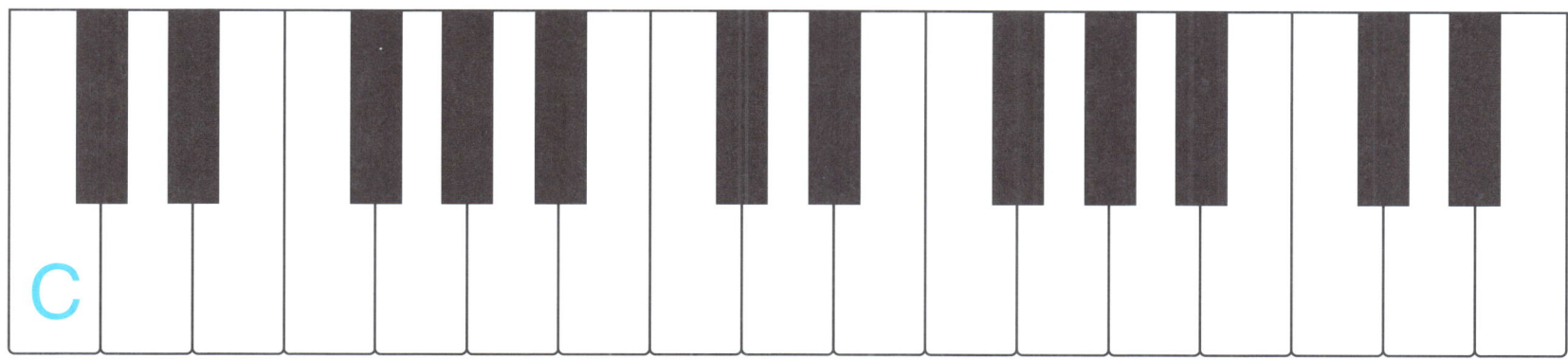

Improvise your own piece.

1. Choose one of the C D E groups on your piano and place your hands in the *Party Cat* position. Make your own piece using the keys pictured here:

2. Play along as you listen to the accompaniment to *Party Cat*.  36

3. Make up more pieces as you play along with the accompaniment for *Balloon Ride*.  34
Just remember to stay in the *Party Cat* position.

Make a Party Game!

The Party Cat (bad cat!) mixed up the keys on the next page so you can't play his song. See if you can put them back in order.

1. Cut out the cards and write the name of each key in the box on the back.

2. Arrange the cards on the music rack of your piano in the order that matches the words:

   "Rock 'n' roll is where it's at"

3. Practise naming the keys on your C D E flash cards.
   How fast can you name them without a mistake?

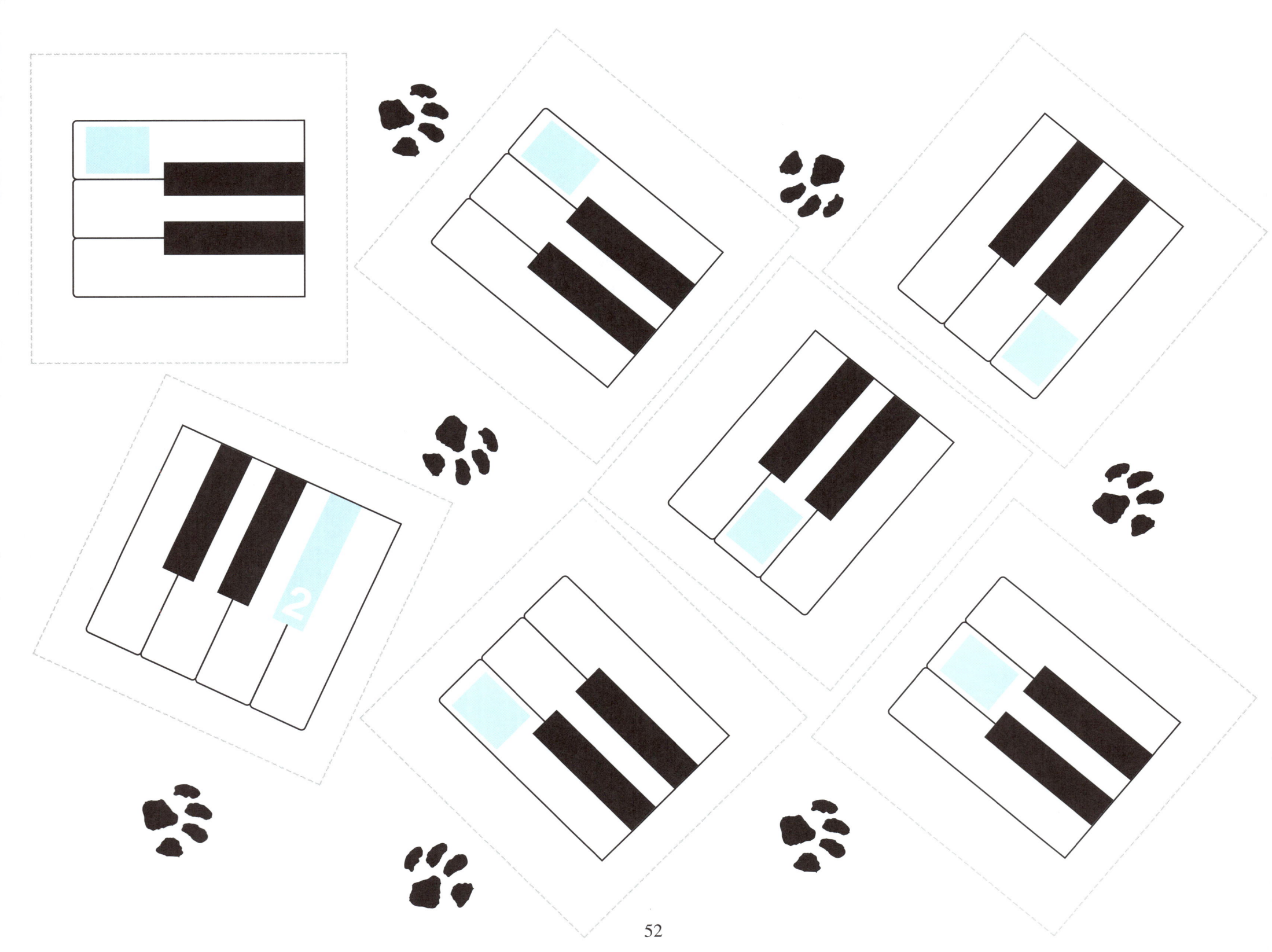

F G A B GROUPS

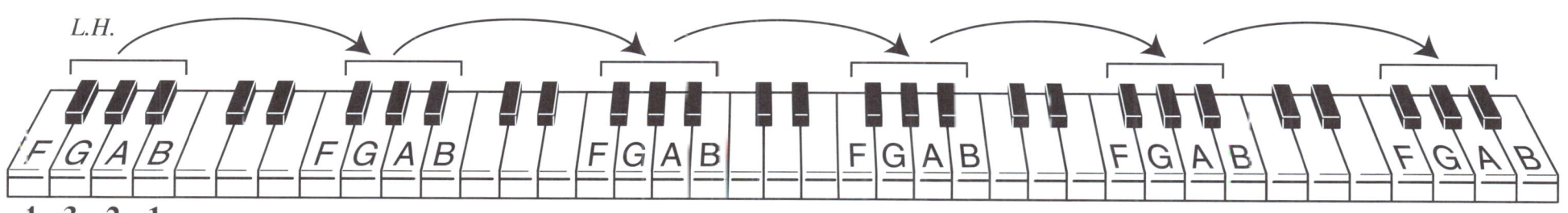

With your left hand, start at the low end of the keyboard and play the
F G A B groups with individual fingers 4-3-2-1 going up the keyboard.

Now explore the keyboard,
playing the F G A B groups
with your right hand using
fingers 1-2-3-4.

F G A B Groups
(Activity Page)

1. Circle the sets of three black keys.
2. Write the F G A B letter names on the white keys.
3. Colour the F's yellow, the G's purple, the A's orange, and the B's brown.

My Own Song
On F G A B

With your left or right hand, choose any F G A B group in the upper part of the piano.

Listen and feel the pulse as your teacher plays the accompaniment below. When you are ready, play F G A B. Experiment by playing B A G F.

Mix the letters any way you want and make up your own song.

Have fun!

Accompaniment 37

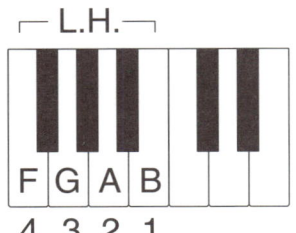

Monster Under My Bed

Phillip Keveren

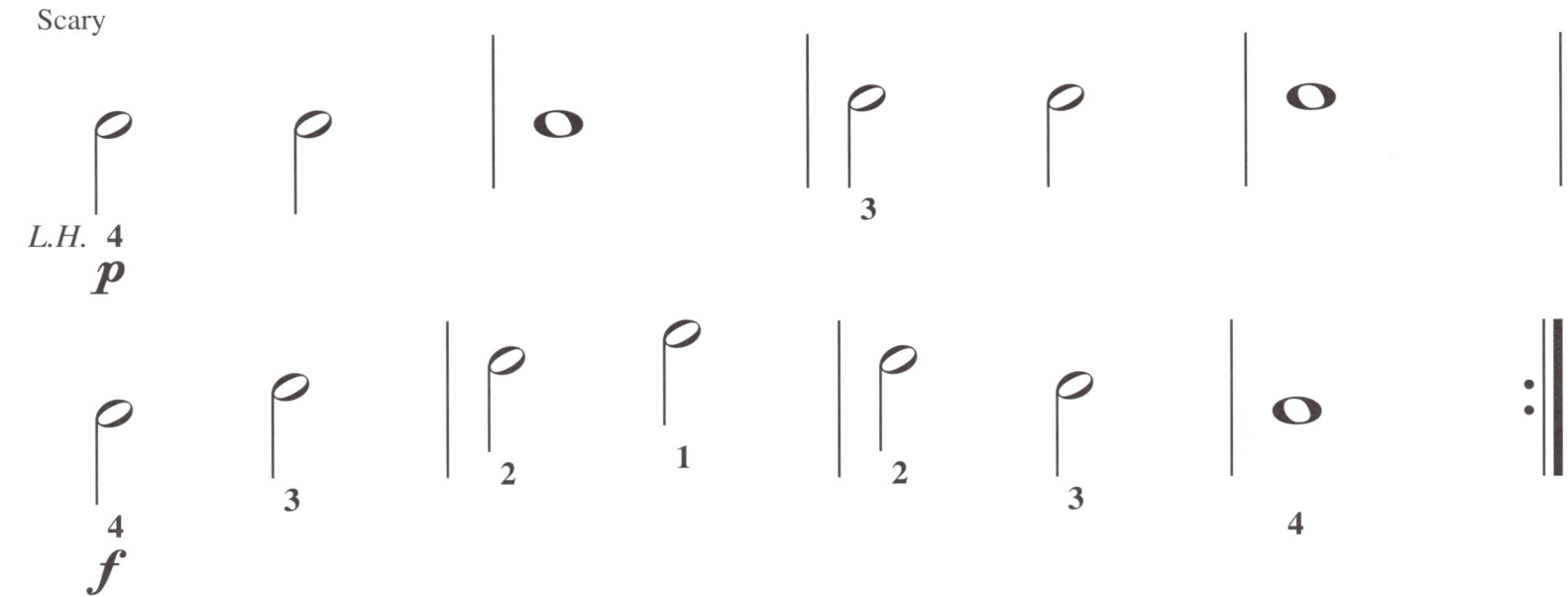

With accompaniment, student starts here:

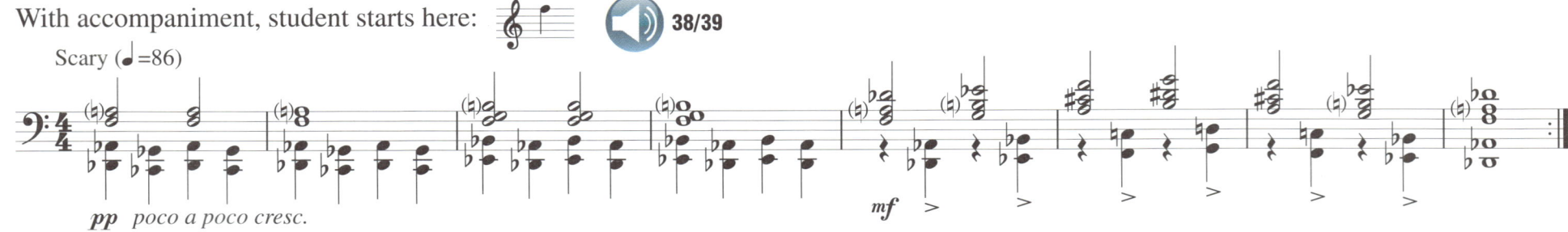

Finding F G A B on the Keyboard

Spike is taking a taxi to his house at the end of Keyboard Lane.
Help the taxi driver follow Spike's directions to his house.

1. Circle the sets of three black keys.

2. Drive to the first F and colour it yellow.

3. Drive to the next F and colour it yellow.

4. Drive to the next A and colour it orange.

5. Drive to the next G and colour it purple.

6. Drive to the next B and colour it brown.

7. Drive to the next G and colour it purple.

8. Drive to the next A and colour it orange.

9. Drive to the next F and colour it yellow.

10. Drive to the next B and colour it brown.

Hooray! Spike's home!

L.H.
R.H.
MIDDLE
2 3
F G A B
4 3 2 1

TAXI
TAXI
TAXI
TAXI

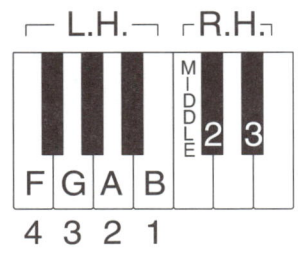

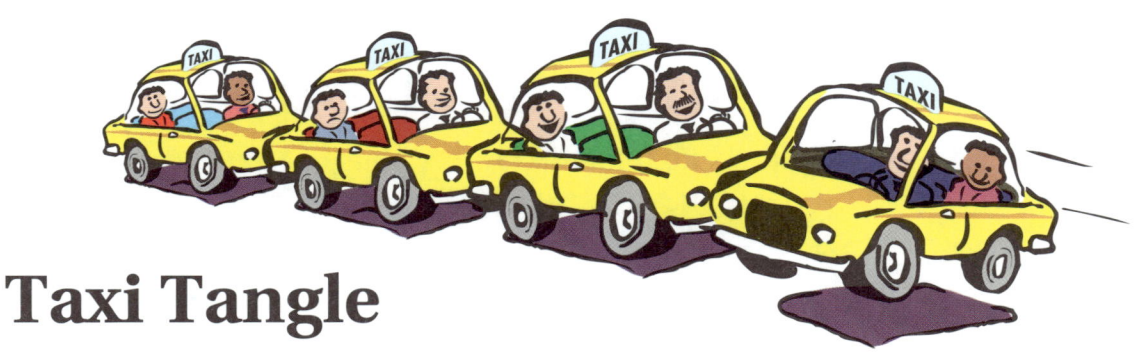

Taxi Tangle

Phillip Keveren

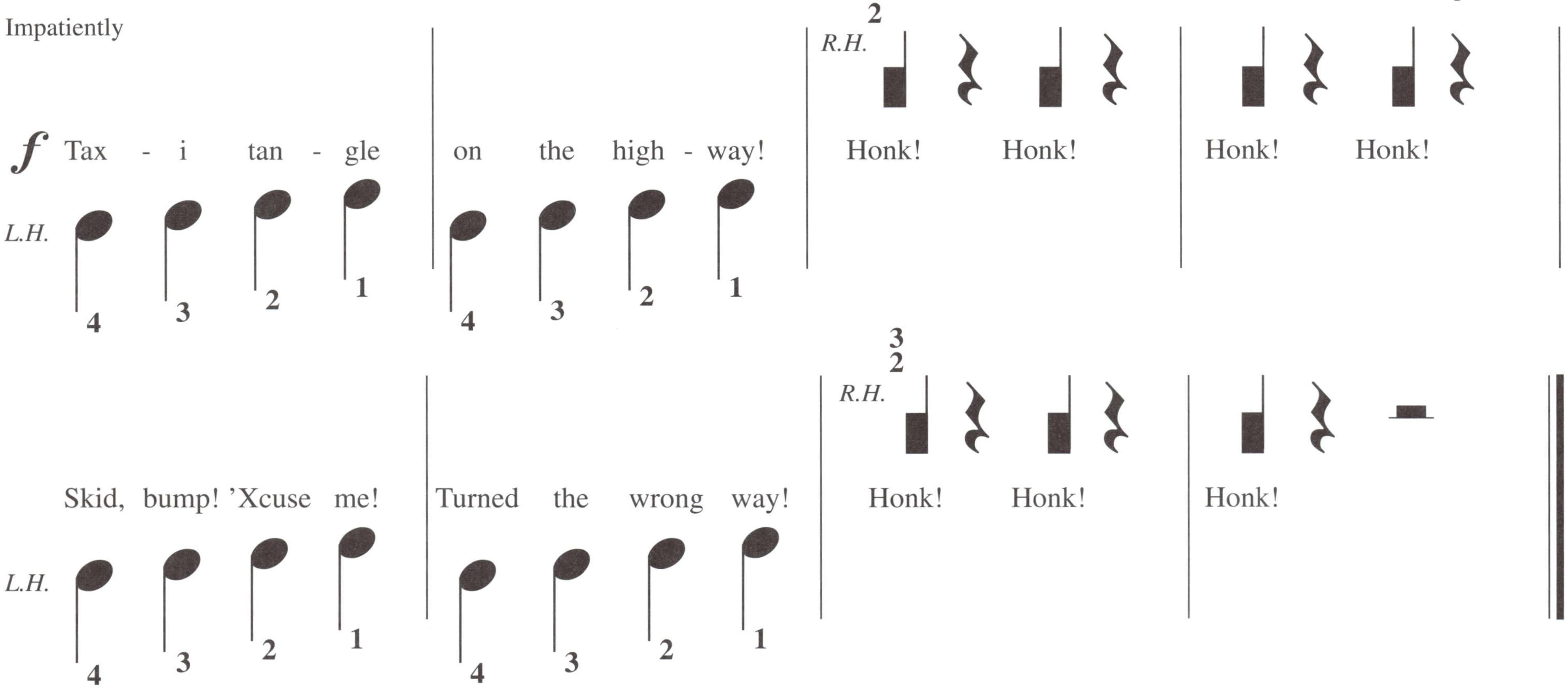

Impatiently
f Tax - i tan - gle on the high - way!
L.H. 4 3 2 1 4 3 2 1
R.H. 3 2
Honk! Honk! Honk! Honk!
Skid, bump! 'Xcuse me! Turned the wrong way!
L.H. 4 3 2 1 4 3 2 1
R.H. 3 2
Honk! Honk! Honk!

With accompaniment, student starts here: 40/41

Impatiently (♩ = 140)
mf

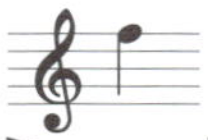

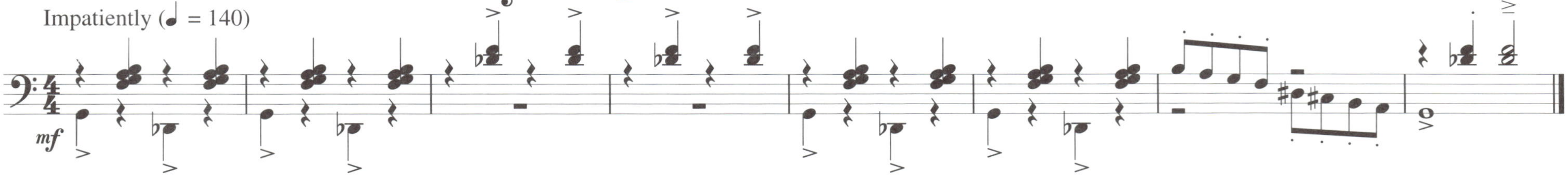

L.H.
R.H.
MIDDLE
2
3
F G A B
4 3 2 1

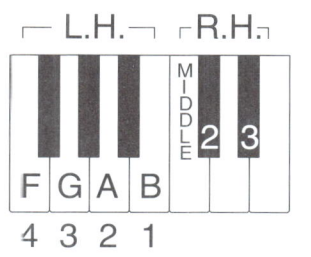

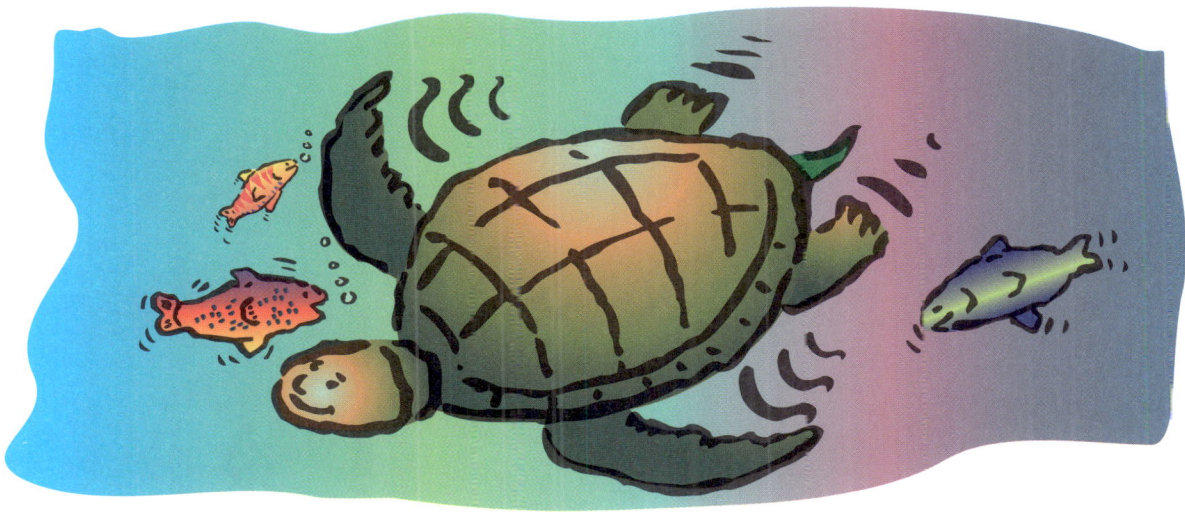

Undersea Voyage

Mysteriously

Phillip Keveren

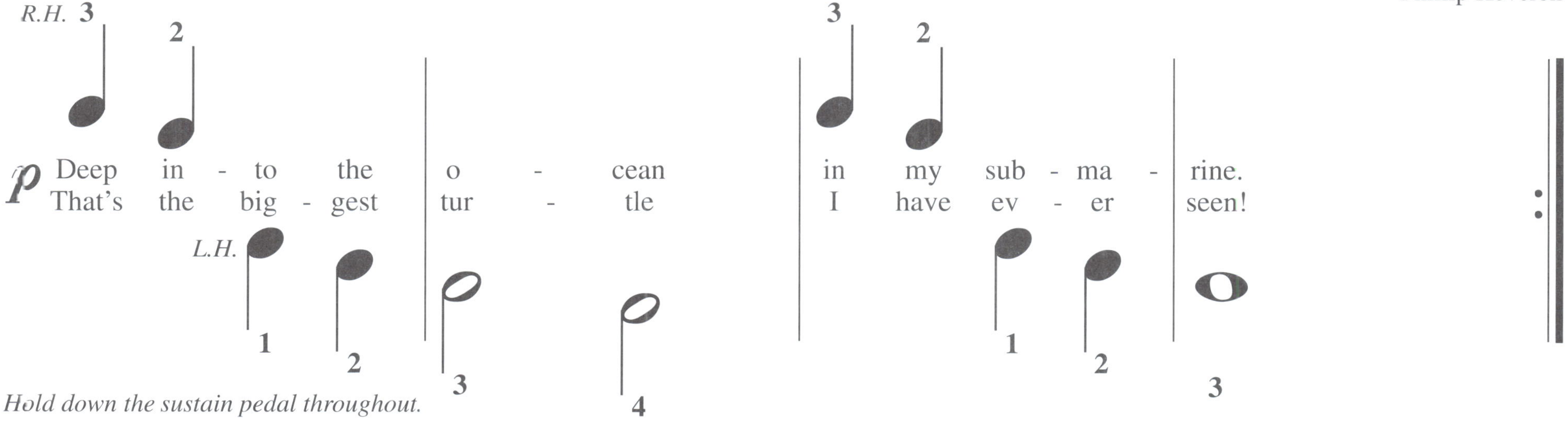

R.H. 3 2
p
Deep in - to the o - cean in my sub - ma - rine.
That's the big - gest tur - tle I have ev - er seen!
L.H.
1 2 3 4 1 2 3

Hold down the sustain pedal throughout.

With accompaniment, student starts here: 42/43

Mysteriously (♩ = 120)
R.H.
pp
L.H.
1.
2.

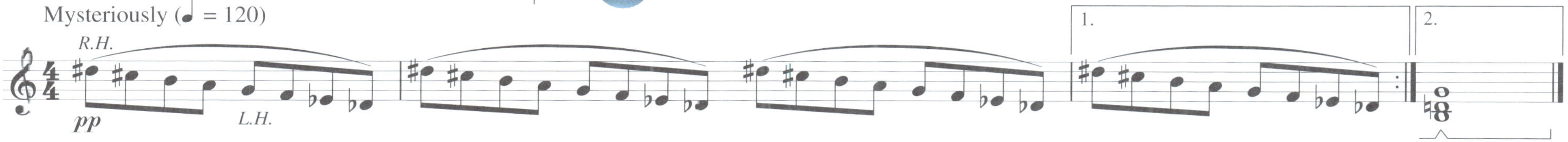

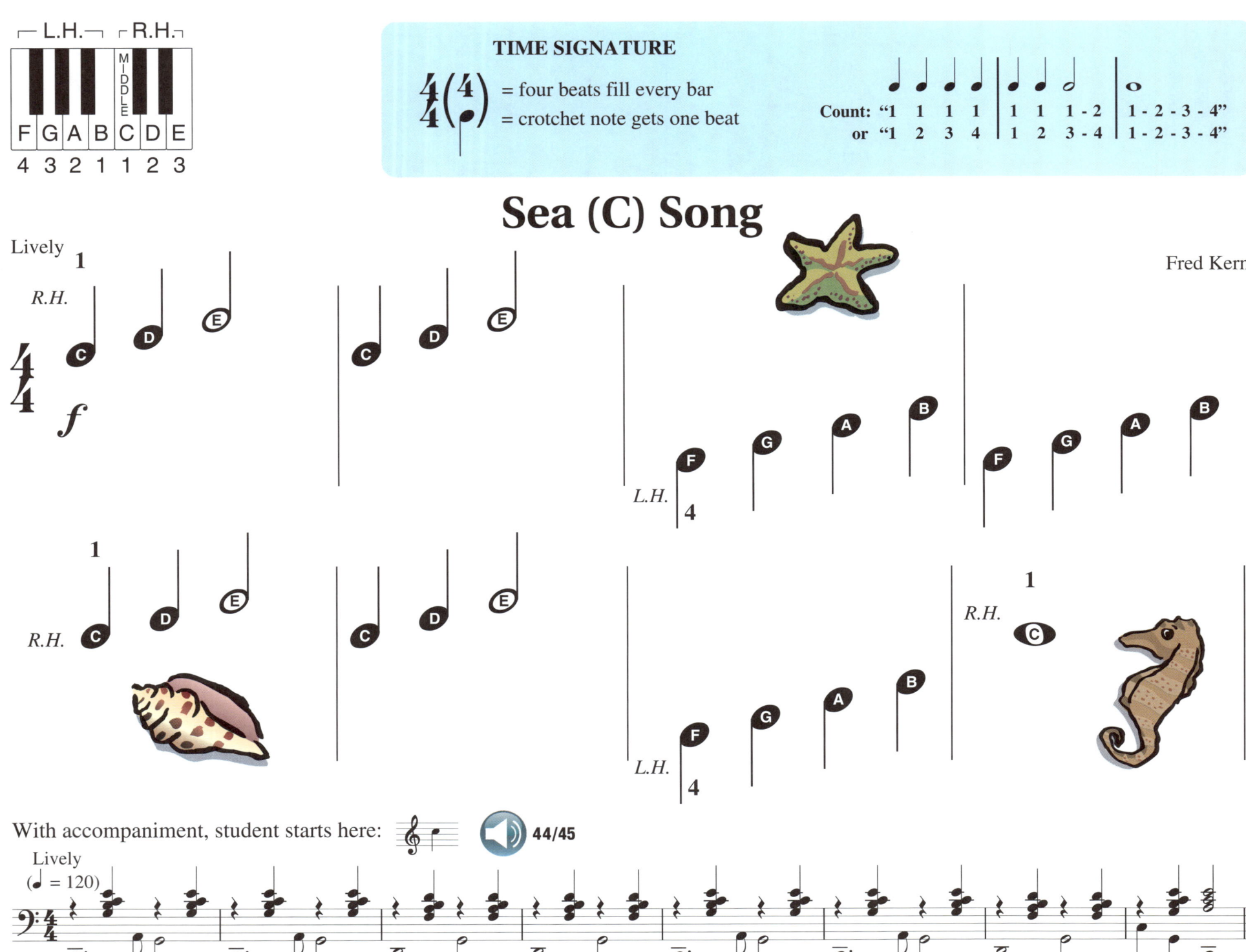

New Position

L.H.
R.H.
MIDDLE
A
C
D
2
2 3

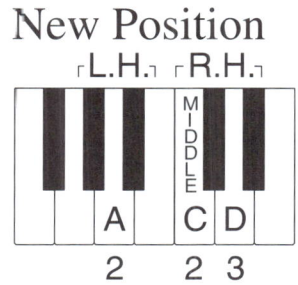

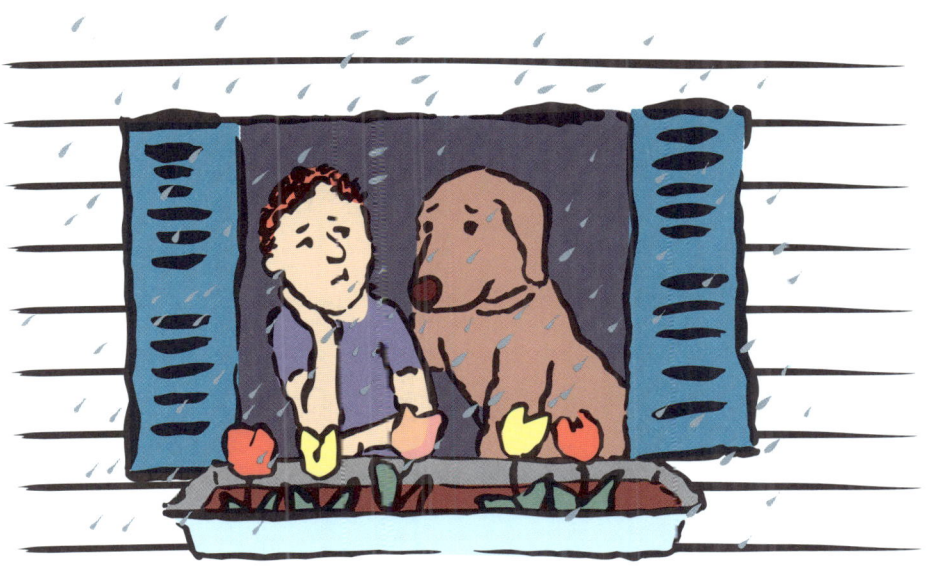

Rain, Rain, Go Away

Steady

Folk Tune

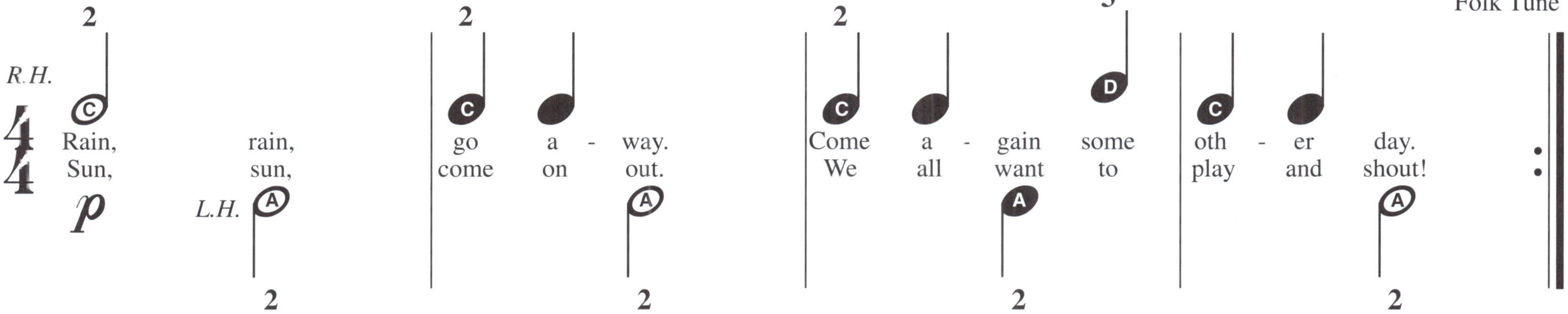

R.H.
L.H.
p
Rain, rain, go a - way. Come a - gain some oth - er day.
Sun, sun, come on out. We all want to play and shout!

With accompaniment, student starts here: 46/47

Steady (♩ = 120)

1.
2.
p

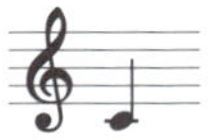

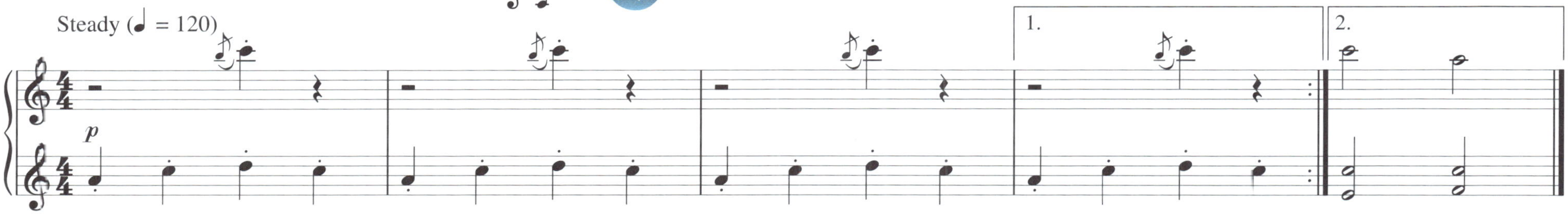

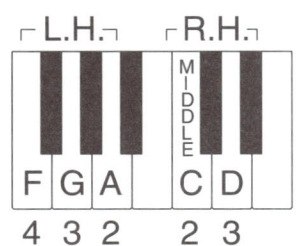

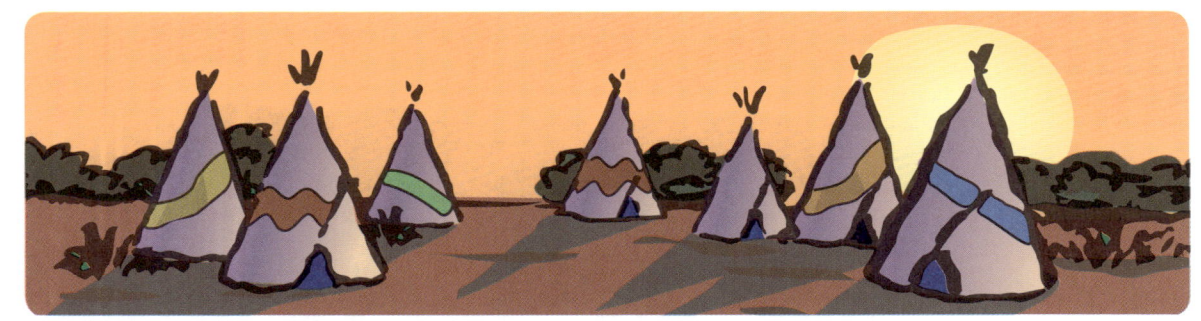

Dakota Melody

With a steady beat

Native American

With accompaniment, student starts here:

48/49

With a steady beat (♩ = 120)

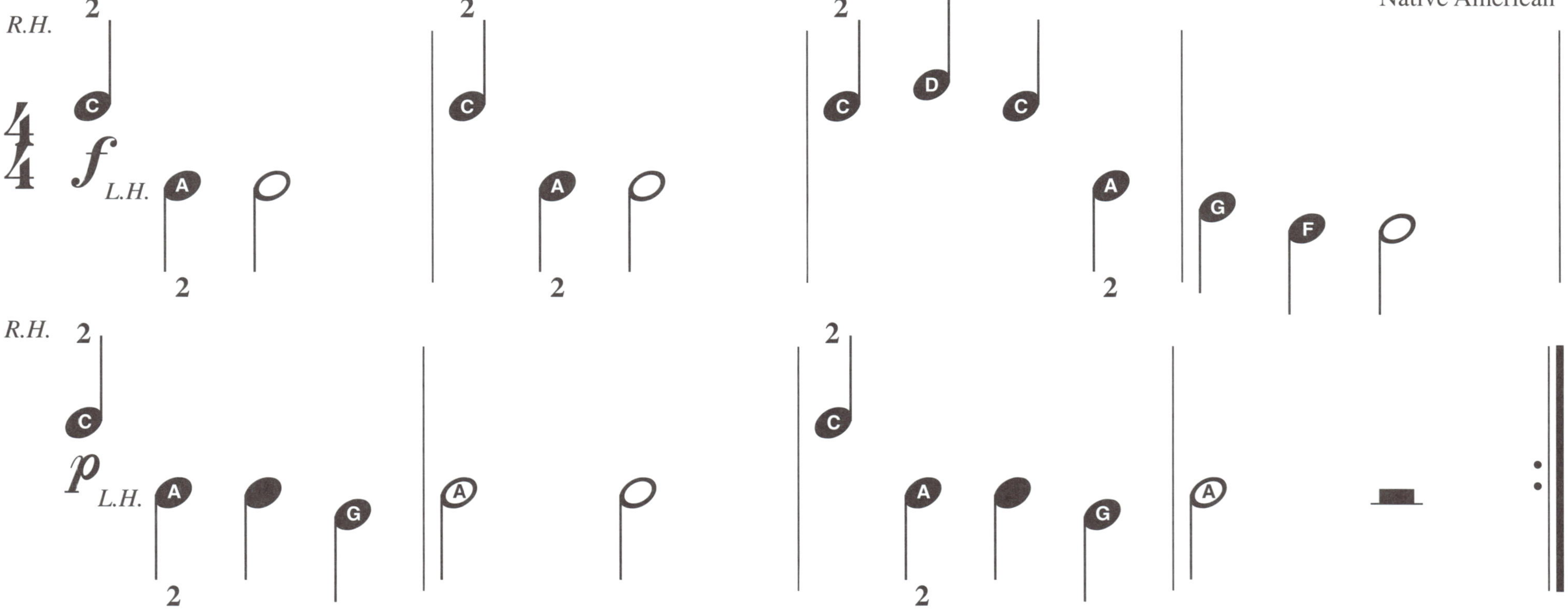

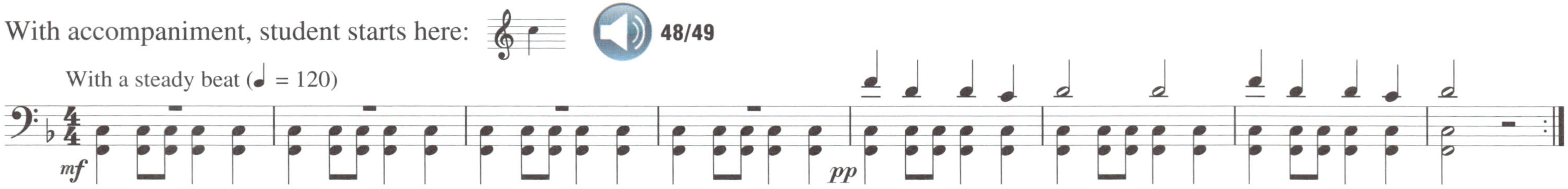

LOUD or *Soft?*
forte – f piano – p

Imagine the way each picture sounds.
Write p for soft or f for loud in the box below each picture.

Naming Notes on the Keyboard

Find the coloured keys that match the coloured boxes below.
To complete this story, write the letter names
of the keys in the coloured boxes.

K[A]ti[E] and M[A]rk s[A]t on th[E] por[C]h,

playin[G] musi[C] [G]ames.

Soon th[E]ir da[D]'s voi[C]e spok[E] to th[E]m [B]oth,

[C]allin[G] out th[E]ir n[A]m[E]s.

"[B]rin[G] me th[E] pap[E]r i[F] you will,"

he asked from 'round the door.

Yet both of the children, not wanting to stop,

played just a minute more.

When finally they finished and looked for the paper,

no sign of it could they see,

Only empty green grass with fresh muddy paw prints,

where do you think it could be?   Who took the paper?

Spike got it.

Quiet Night

Bill Boyd

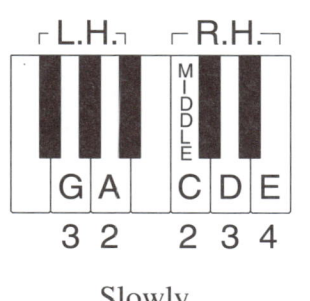

Knock-Knock Joke

Guatemalan

Listen & Respond

 52

Knock-Knock Joke
(Activity Page)

As you listen to *Knock-Knock Joke*, follow the score in your lesson book and knock on the piano cabinet with your right hand every time you see:

Read & Discover

1. The music detective has come knocking at your door to ask you some questions about *Knock-Knock Joke*. Study the score and write your answers to the questions in the boxes below.

   Which finger always plays the R.H. crotchet notes?

   What note does the R.H. play?

   Which L.H. finger do you skip in bar 1?

   Which finger plays G in bar 2?

2. Now the detective wants you to write the letter names of the missing notes in the boxes below. Add the finger numbers in the blanks below them.

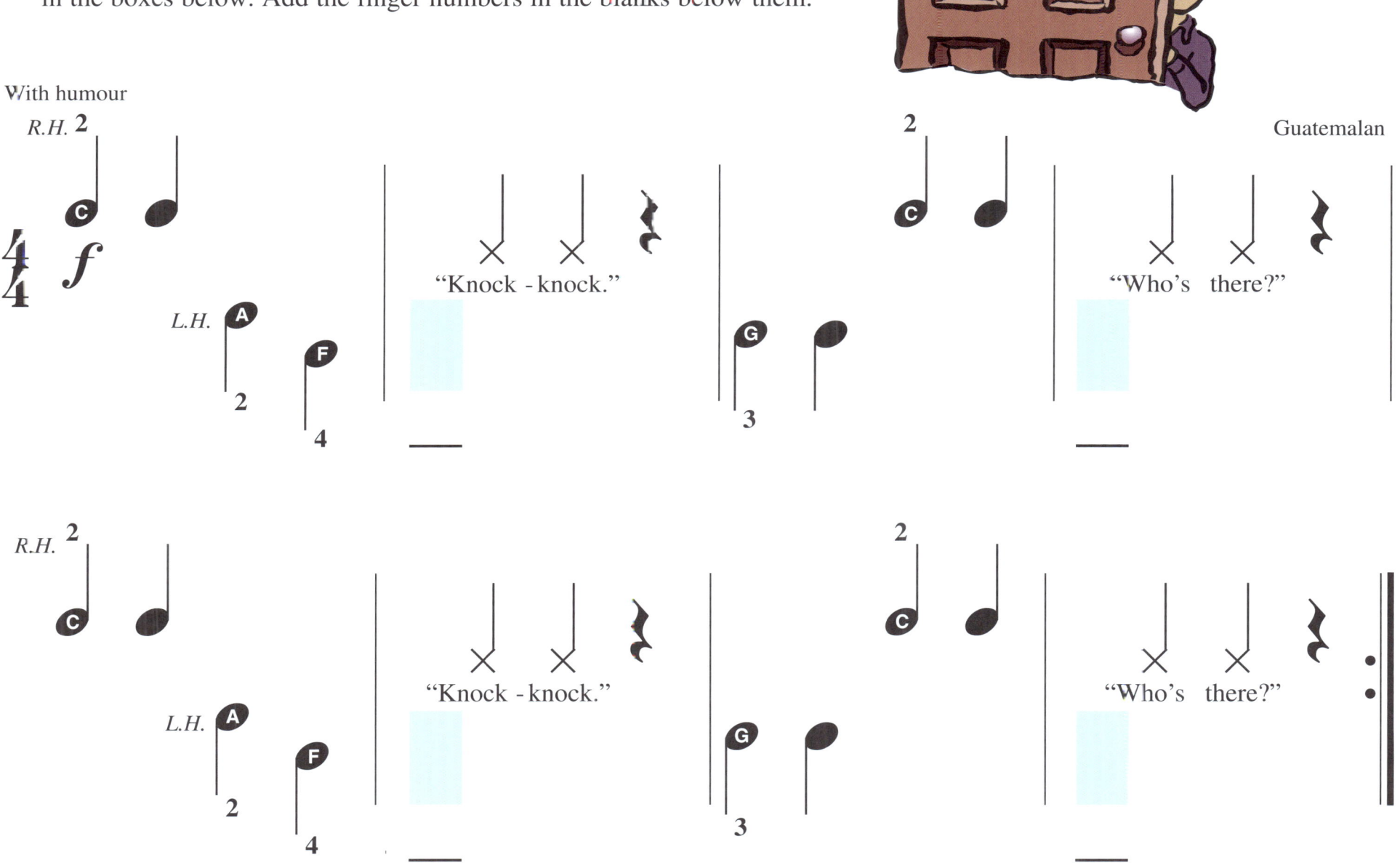

Guatemalan

3. Tap your foot on ♩ ♩ as you play the song!

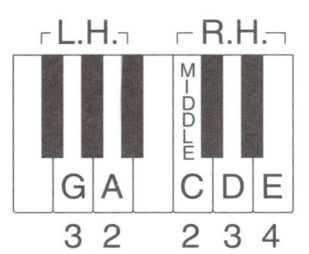

Old MacDonald Had A Band

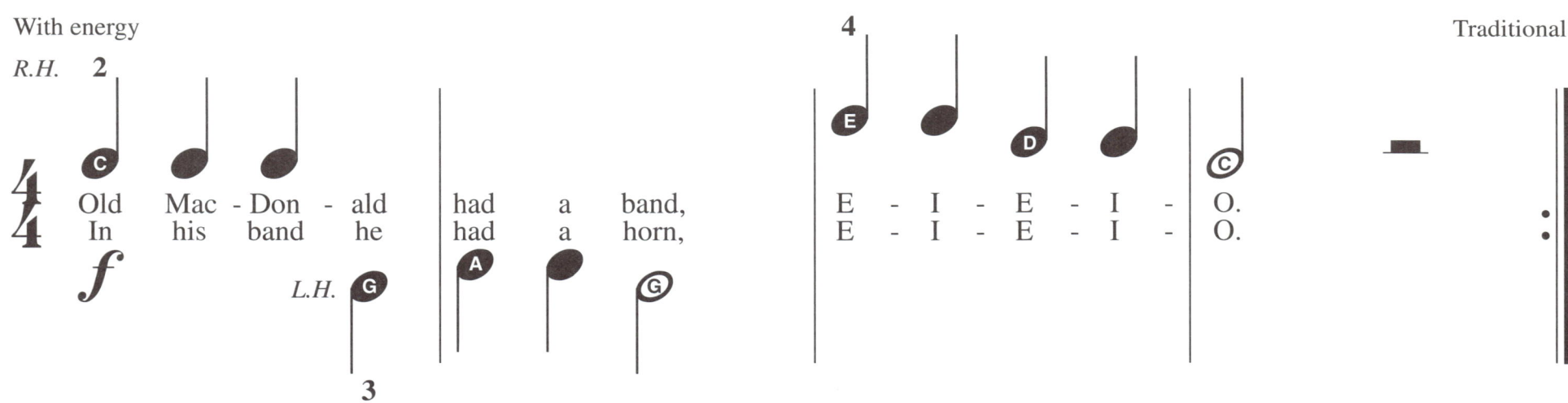

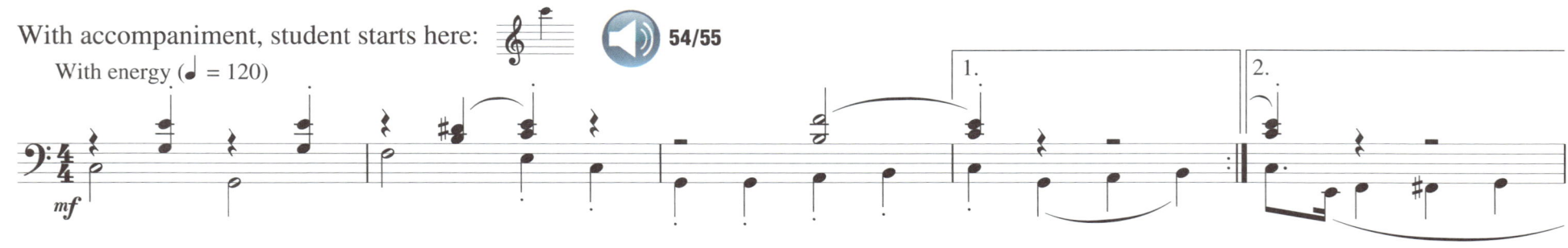

Rhythm Jam

When Old MacDonald's band began rehearsing music for its next show, they discovered that some of the bars weren't complete.

Circle the one note or rest in the blue box that will complete each bar.

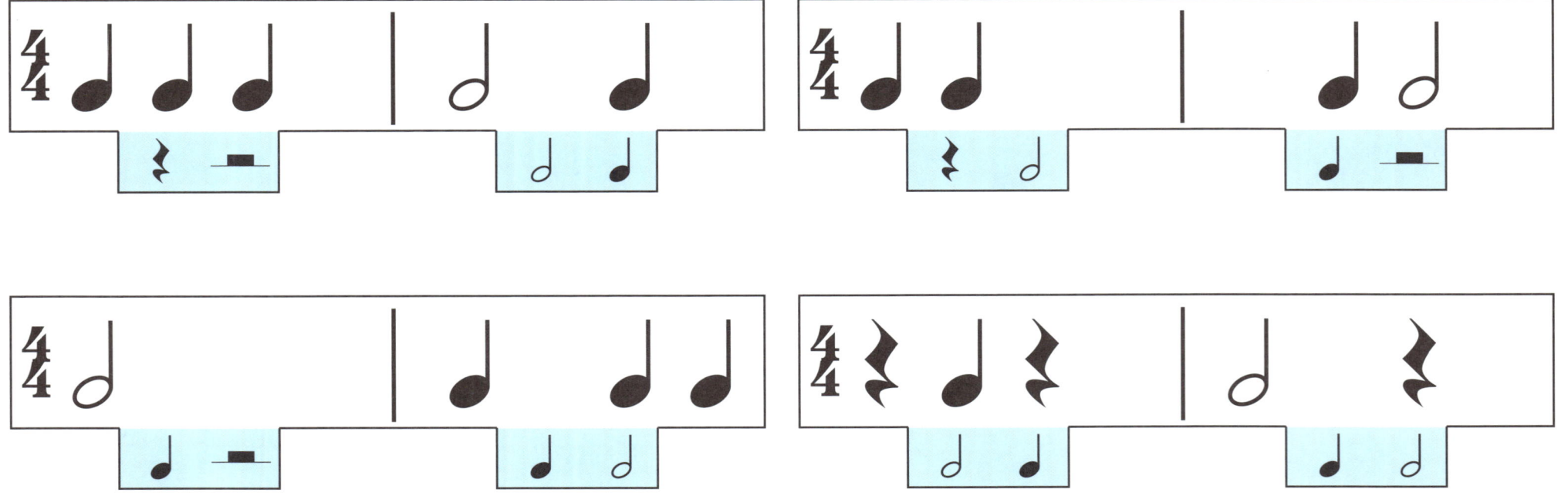

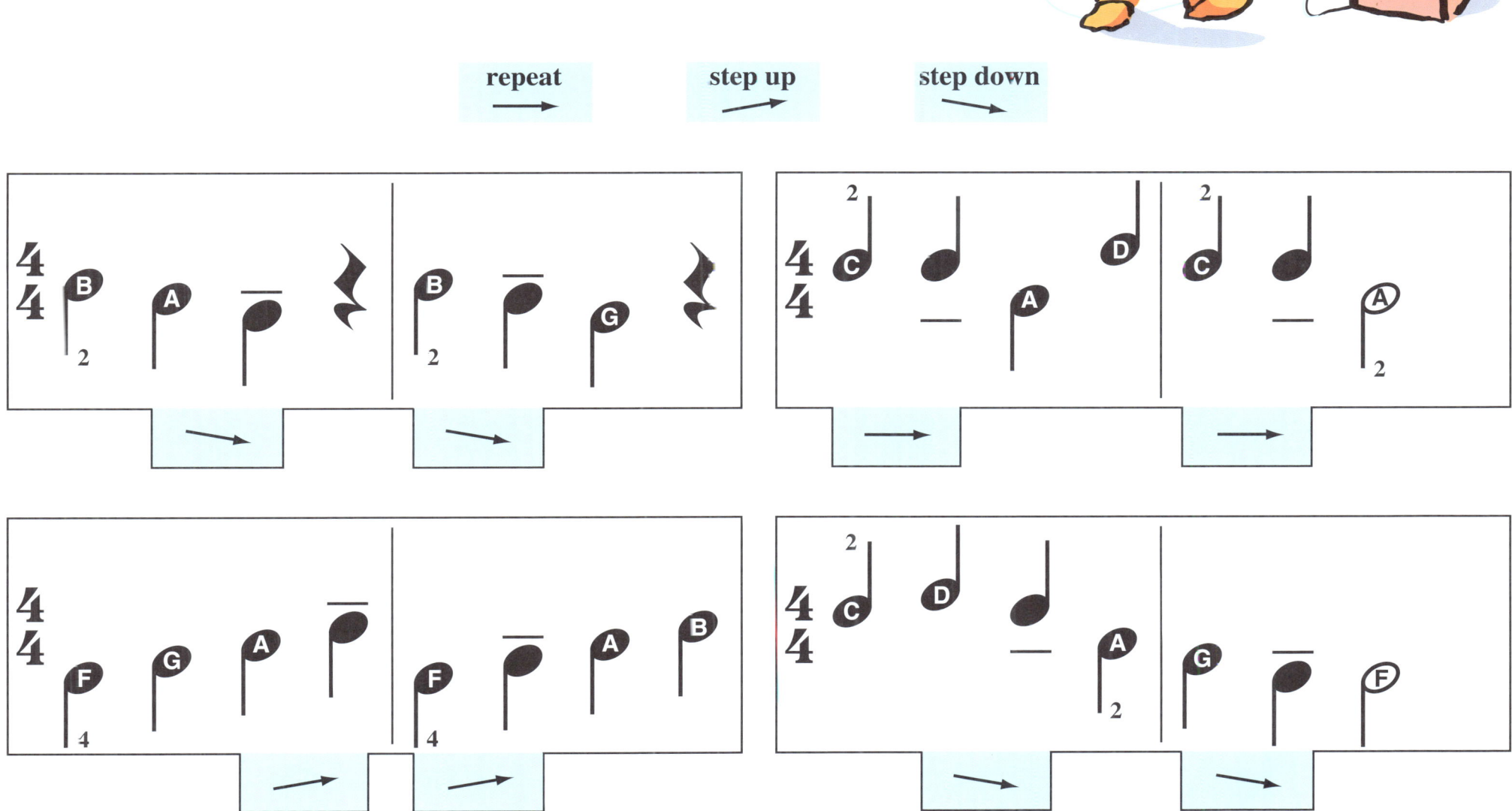

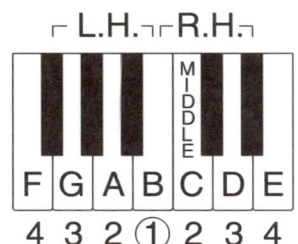

Playing Catch

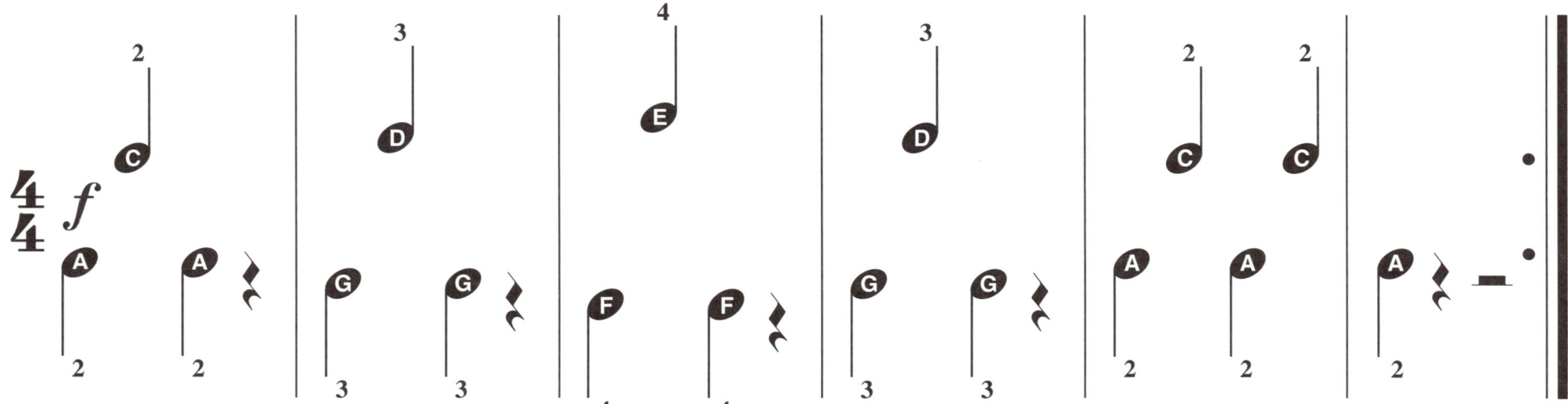

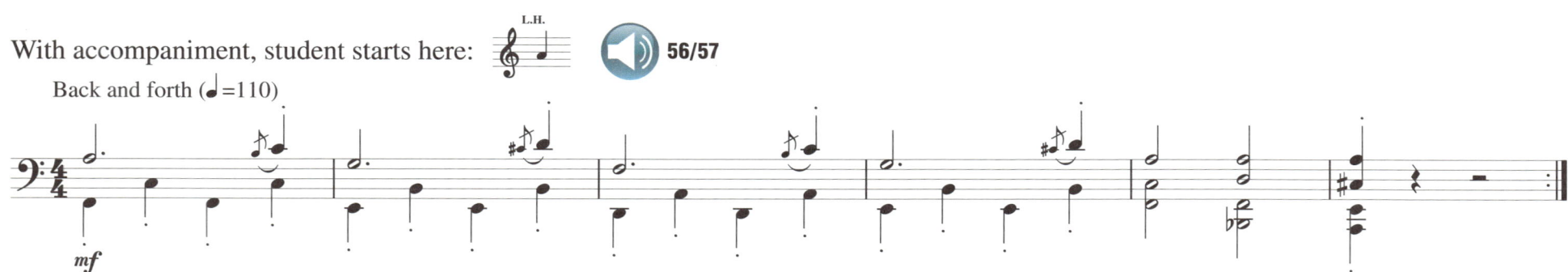

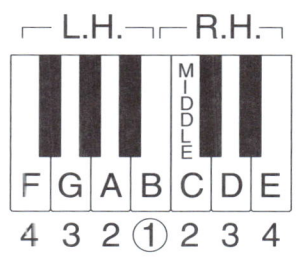

Popcorn

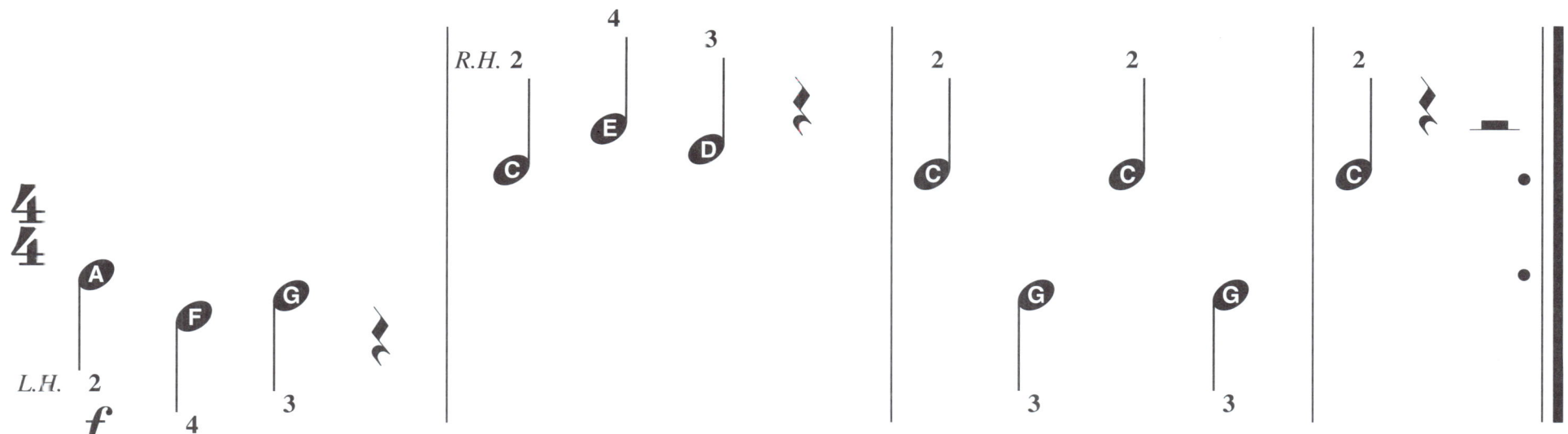

With accompaniment, student starts here: 58/59

Bouncy (♩=110)

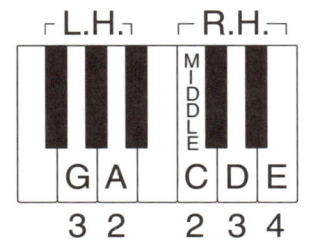

Bear Dance

Somewhat heavily

Christos Tsitsaros

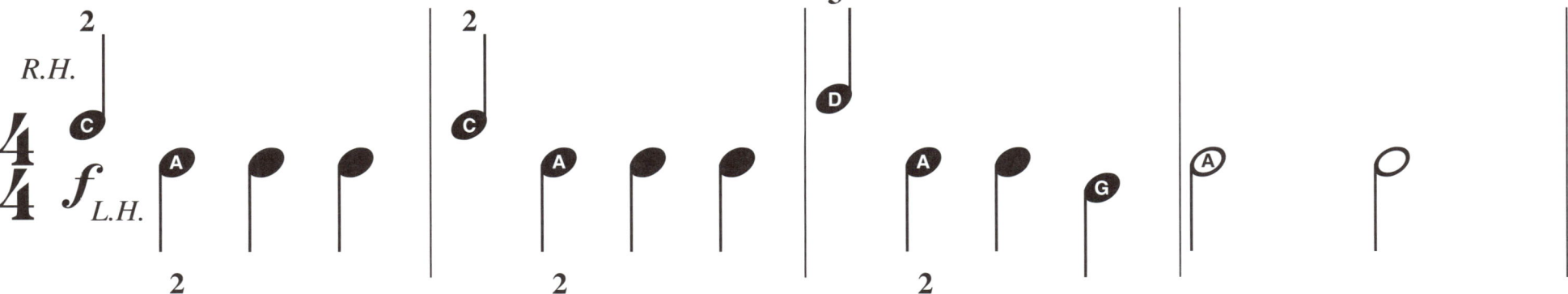
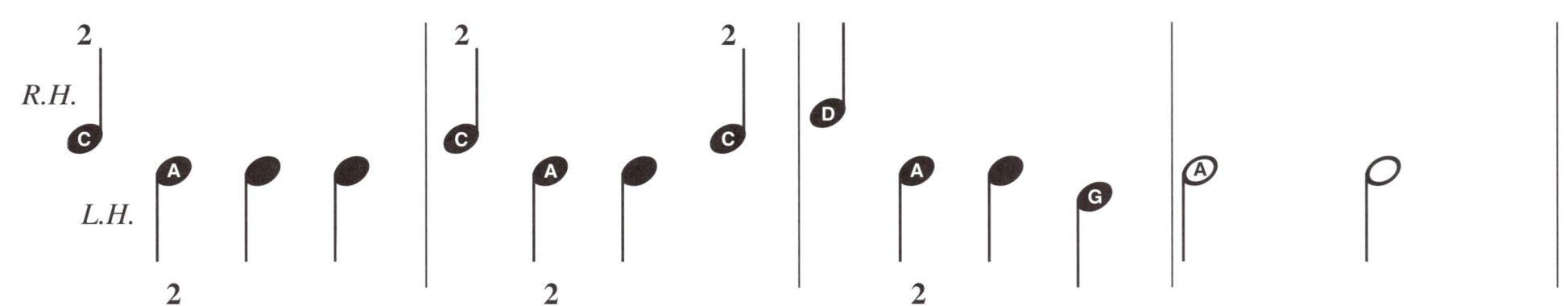

With accompaniment, student starts here:
Somewhat heavily (♩= 150)

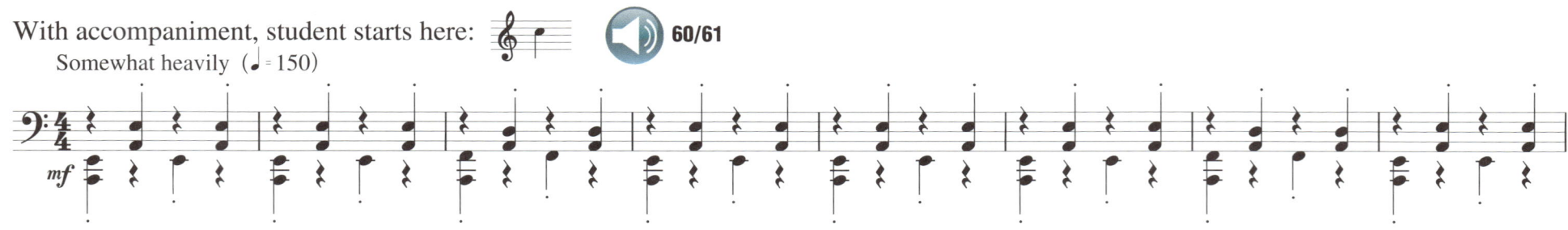

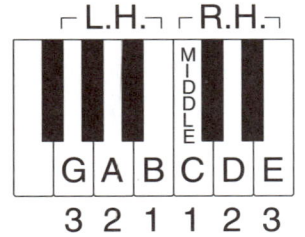

Stomp Dance

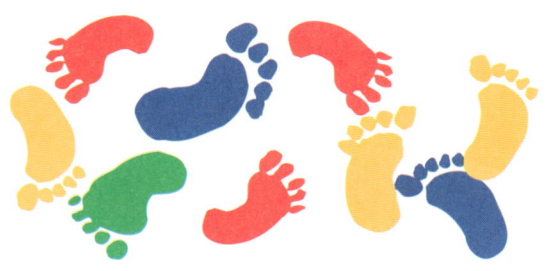

Lively, with a steady beat

Carol Klose

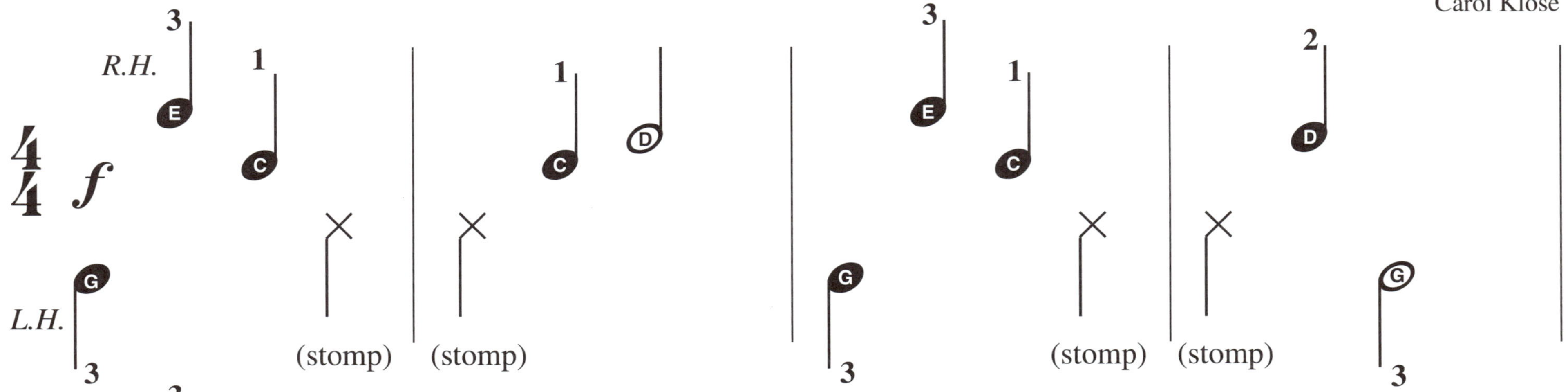

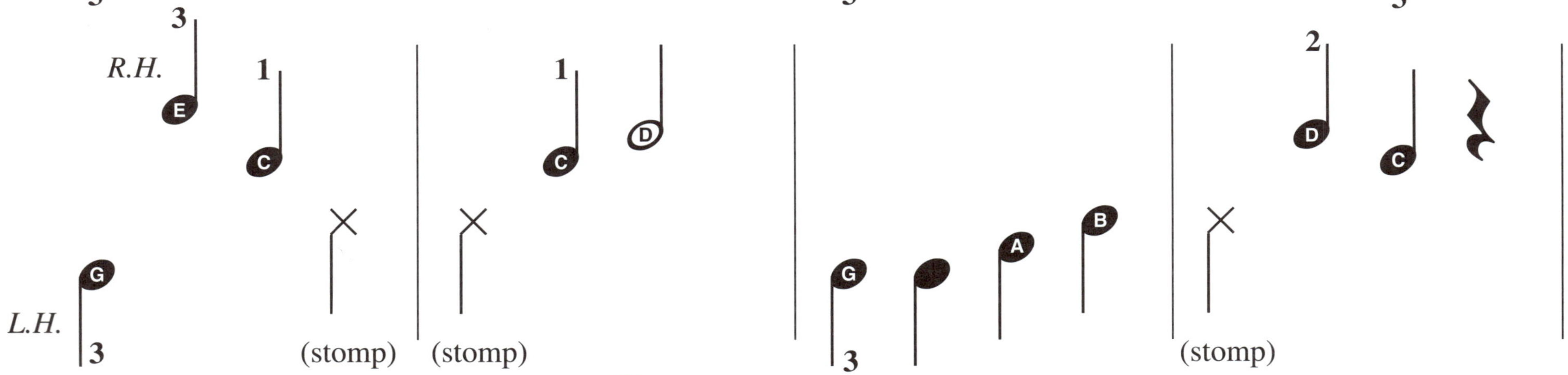

With accompaniment, student starts here: 62/63

Lively, with a steady beat (♩♩ = ♩♪ triplet) (♩ = 120)

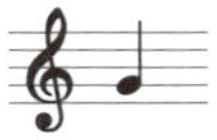

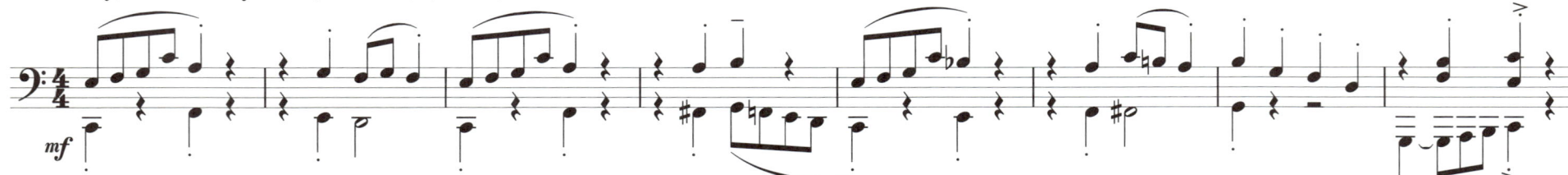

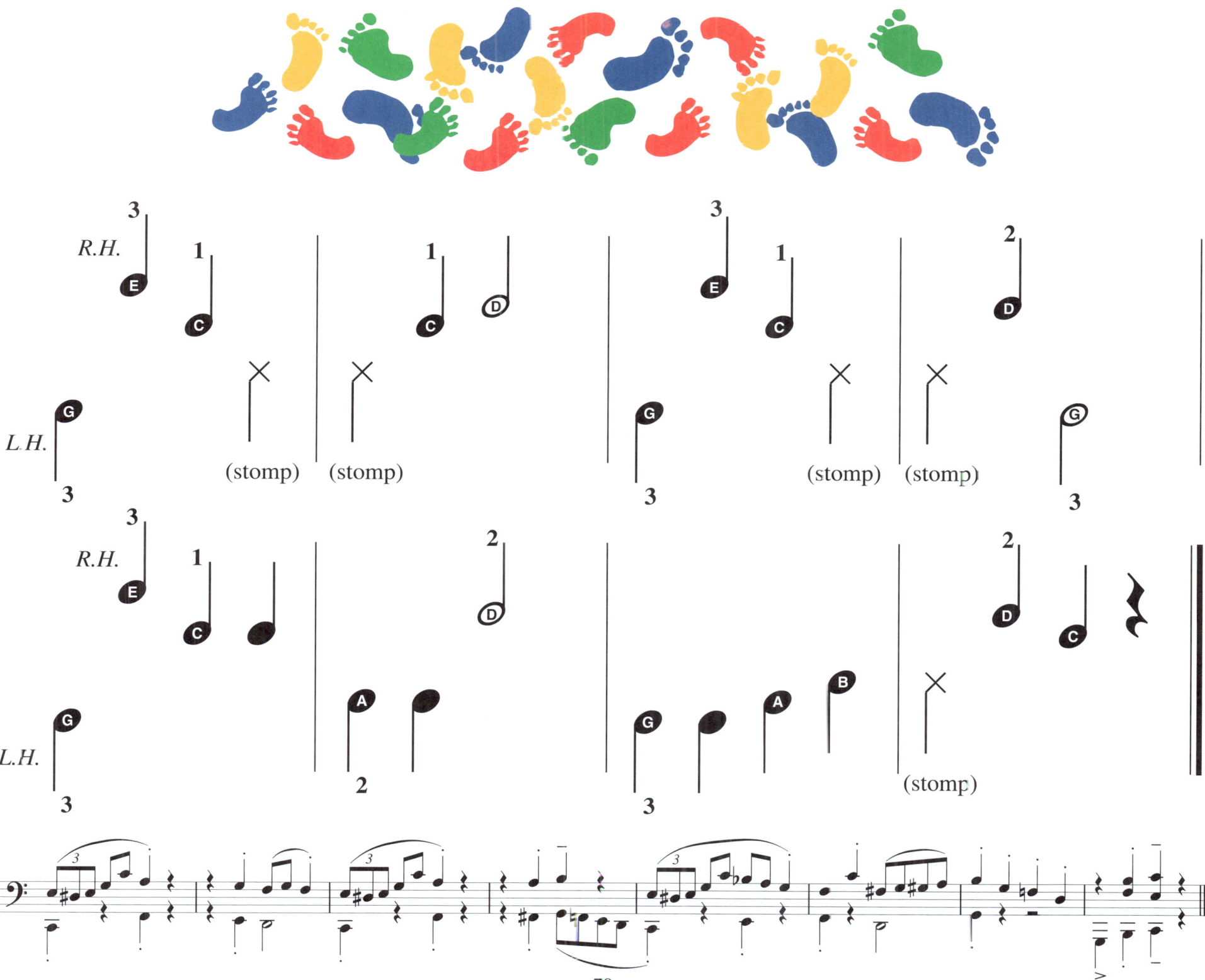

AWARD CERTIFICATE

____

HAS SUCCESSFULLY COMPLETED
HAL LEONARD ALL-IN-ONE
PIANO LESSONS, BOOK A
AND
IS HEREBY PROMOTED TO
BOOK B

______________________ ____________
TEACHER DATE

HAL•LEONARD®

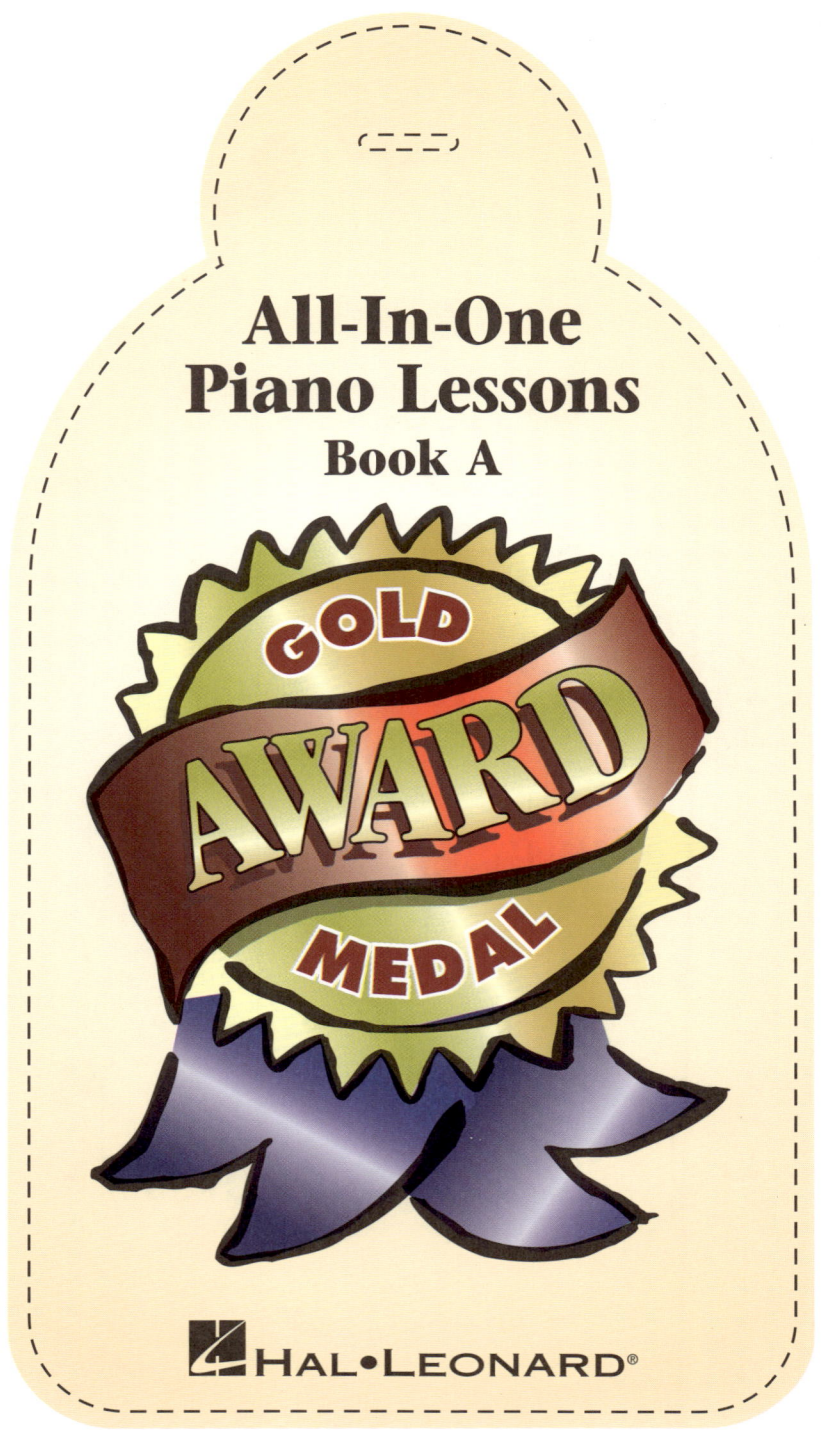

All-In-One Piano Lessons
Book A

HAL•LEONARD®

Cut-out may be fitted over student's shirt button.